MW00462567

WSJ BEST
CHOOSE YOURSE

THE

RICH

EMPLOYEE

JAMES

ALTUCHER

THE RICH EMPLOYEE

✳

COPYRIGHT © JAMES ALTUCHER

FIRST EDITION: SEPTEMBER 2015

ALL RIGHTS RESERVED.

No part of this publication may be reproduced, stored in or introduced into a retrieval system, or transmitted, in any form or by any means (electronically, mechanical, photocopying, recording or otherwise), without the prior written permission of both the copyright owner and the publisher of this book.

Re-selling through electronic outlets (like Amazon, Barnes and Nobles or E-bay) without permission of the publisher is illegal and punishable by law.

The scanning, uploading, and distribution of this book via the Internet or via any other means without the permission of the publisher is illegal and punishable by law.

Please purchase only authorized editions and no not participate in or encourage electronic piracy of copyrightable materials.

Your support of the author's right is appreciated.

ISBN-13: 9781517088729 | ISBN-10: 1517088720

COVER DESIGN AND INTERIOR LAYOUT BY: ERIN TYLER
E-BOOK DESIGN BY: IAN CLAUDIUS
EXECUTIVE PRODUCER AND MANAGING EDITOR:
CLAUDIA AZULA ALTUCHER

CHOOSE YOURSELF
MEDIA LLC.

CONTENTS

DEDICATION 7

WHO IS THIS BOOK FOR? 8

THE RICH EMPLOYEE MENTALITY 12

START THE ROAD TOWARDS BECOMING A RICH EMPLOYEE EXACTLY

WHERE YOU ARE 22

10 THINGS A RICH EMPLOYEE DOES IF SHE OR HE HAS JUST BEEN FIRED . . . 24

10 THINGS A RICH EMPLOYEE WILL DO IF SHE IS HIRED TODAY 28

10 REASONS A RICH EMPLOYEE WILL STAY AT HER OR HIS JOB: FOR NOW . . 36

WHY BE A RICH EMPLOYEE? 44

WHY YOU MUST URGENTLY BECOME A RICH EMPLOYEE, RIGHT NOW 44

HOW TO BE A 'MASTER' OR AT LEAST: THE SMARTEST

'RICH EMPLOYEE' IN THE ROOM 48

THE RICH EMPLOYEE VERSUS THE POOR EMPLOYEE MENTALITY 54

HOW A RICH EMPLOYEE THINKS 54

HOW A POOR EMPLOYEE THINKS 98

HOW TO BECOME A RICH EMPLOYEE 102

THE RICH EMPLOYEE MIRACLE MORNING 102

HOW A RICH EMPLOYEE CREATES HIS OR HER SIDE HUSTLE 108

HOW DOES A RICH EMPLOYEE HANDLE WHEN OTHERS GET

JEALOUS AND TRASH HER OR HIM? 118

HABITS OF THE MENTALLY STRONG RICH EMPLOYEE 126

HABITS OF THE POOR EMPLOYEE 138

How The Rich Employee Learns. 146

A Rich Employee Is Always Learning 146

Frequent and Important Questions Rich Employees Have 156

How Does A Rich Employee Deal With A Crappy Boss

While In Transition? 156

Why Is It Especially Important For Women Rich Employees

to Become Idea Machines? 162

Just One Thing to Do 174

How Does A Rich Employee Master New Skills? 178

How Does A Rich Employee Transform Anger Into "What Works"? . .190

Is There A "Right Way" To Ask For Things That The

Rich Employee Utilizes? 196

As A Rich Employee How Do I Know If I Should Take a

Job In A Start-Up? 204

Resources for The Rich Employee 210

Create A Choose Yourself Meet-up In Your Town 210

How To Run A Choose Yourself Meet-Up 212

Suggested Websites Where The Rich Employee Can

Learn New Skills 222

Book Suggestions 224

In Conclusion 228

Books in The *Choose Yourself* Family 230

About The Author 232

Contact 234

DEDICATION

There are 100,000,000 employees in the United States.

3,000,000,000 employees worldwide.

This book is dedicated to all of them.

WHO IS THIS BOOK FOR?

·············· ✳ ··············

When I first wrote *"Choose Yourself"*, many people wrote me and said, "what if I'm not an entrepreneur".

Not everyone is an entrepreneur. I've been an employee as often as I've been an entrepreneur.

"Choose Yourself" was when I was at my worst moment, not only financially but physically, emotionally, mentally, and spiritually.

It's how I recovered. It's how I literally saved my life. I called it my *daily practice* and I described in detail how I used it to not only survive but thrive.

It doesn't matter if you are an entrepreneur. Or an employee. You can choose yourself and thrive and change the world. Every day I bring my energy into the world by first concentrating on how I can build up the energy inside of myself.

Having a "Rich Employee" mindset is critical to creating the life you want to live, whether you work for yourself or you work for, or with others.

Corporations filled with "rich employees" will change the world. People with a Rich Employee mindset will first choose themselves and from that vantage point, do whatever they want.

This book is for people who want to do what they want. Individuals who want to pursue their life's dreams. And for the people who work with them and are inspired by them.

More specifically, this book is for:

Managers

Your success is determined by the success of the people who work for you. If your employees understand the company, the brand, your needs, your boss's needs, so much so that they see their own futures stapled to satisfying those needs, then you will succeed.

Ultimately a manager is guiding a ship. You can't do anything about the weather. You just have to make sure everyone is doing what they are supposed to do to take advantage of the good weather and to survive when there is bad weather.

The Poor Employee will jump ship when there's bad weather. Will do a mediocre job when there is good weather, and is always planning mutiny.

The Rich Employee wants to help you get to your destination and beyond. A culture of the Rich Employee Mindset will create abundance for your group and everyone in your company, including customers, and shareholders will take notice and see it.

Employees

Many people think in terms of "Should I stay at this job or should I be an entrepreneur?"

It doesn't matter. You get out of a situation exactly what you bring into it.

If you bring in the Rich Employee mindset then you come out rich (in health, mind, body, bank account).

If you bring in the Poor Employee mindset you come out poor.

There's the story of the two men who visit a Zen master.

The first man says: "I'm thinking of moving to this town. What's it like?"

The Zen master says: "What was your old town like?"

The first man says: "It was dreadful. Everyone was hateful. I hated it."

The Zen master says: "This town is very much the same. I don't think you should move here."

The first man left and a second man came in.

The second man said: "I'm thinking of moving to this town. What's it like?"

The Zen master said: "What was your old town like?"

The second man said: "It was wonderful. Everyone was friendly and I was happy. Just interested in a change now."

The Zen master said: "This town is very much the same. I think you will like it here."

This book is about becoming the second man. The one who will make the most of any situation. The one who will weave abundance out of any job/location instead of just get by until he is dissatisfied again and is forced to move on.

ENTRENPRENEURS

Why would an entrepreneur read a book about being a Rich Employee?

Being an entrepreneur still means you have a job. It's just that you created the job!

And your job is much more difficult because everyone knows the rate of failure of all startups is 85%! There's no way around that statistic.

I've done due diligence on hundreds of companies. I'm invested in about 30. I've started 20. I've had my 85% failure rate, sometimes very painfully.

I wish I had known the principles outlined in this book.

Often we write about the things that were hardest for us to learn. I had to spend twenty years or more learning these principles in dozens of situations, and by analyzing thousands of other examples.

The Rich Employee morphs into the successful entrepreneur who, in turns, will know how to make his own employees Rich Employees.

This feels good. This creates value and innovation in the world.

This is success.

THE RICH EMPLOYEE MENTALITY

· · · · · · · · · · · · · · · ✳ · · · · · · · · · · · · · · ·

A t some point we wake up.

For me, it could've been the time my father told me that after a year of nursery school, there would be a year of kindergarten, then six years of elementary school, six years of middle school and high school, four years of college, three years of graduate school, and then about forty years of work -Then retirement. "Like grandpa", he said. I was three years old.

Or it could have been the time my boss was screaming at me at work for some small misstep I had taken – and did not know yet that I had just received a job offer from my dream company. Mid-yelling I was able to hold up my hand and say, "It's ok. I quit." That was a good moment.

Another time was when I quit a job to join the company I had started 18 months earlier. Another time was when I realized that I had squandered that company when I sold it and lost all the money.

There's been quite a few times. I went from employee to entrepreneur, back to employee, back to entrepreneur. Never quite getting it. Never quite fully realizing. What was there to realize? That it was over.

The Industrial Revolution had given way to the so-called Knowledge Economy was now giving way to something totally knew, a brand new live child of historical tectonic shifts - *the Idea Economy*. I wasn't always ready for this. I lost my way. Many times I hit my head against the wall and said, "Why is this happening to me AGAIN!?" And the rate at which I was saying this was happening faster and faster. The world was just changing too fast and I didn't understand what to do.

I was scared.

What is the shift?

It can be summed up one way: everything that can be outsourced will be outsourced. Anything that can be replaced with technology will be replaced with technology. All of the readers of this book grew up partly in the industrial economy and partly in the knowledge economy. But industry has become outsourced to either distant parts of the world or eventually to robots. And knowledge is now outsourced as well. Just like monks living in isolated monasteries would toil years over a book and then the Gutenberg press eliminated the need for them, almost any skill - even skills paid for with brutal educations - will be outsourced somewhere. The horse gave way to the car. The VCR gave way to streaming video. Bookstores are giving way to Amazon. Some of it is sad. I miss wandering the aisles of bookstores at the mall. I am nostalgic for arcades with games like Asteroids and Pac-Man. I'm actually nostalgic for the days when we had only three channels and had to find the just-right show to watch to be entertained. I'm nostalgic for boredom and sitting around in my bed and just daydreaming about the future, or bike riding down safe suburban streets, looking for my friends to play with. Sitting at home with my grandparents on a Saturday night, laughing to *"The Golden Girls"* because it was something my grandparents and I bonded together over. Now, kids and their parents spread out with one eye on their phones, one eye on the TV with a billion channels and one eye, who knows where?

To fight the change is silly. It's like saying the sun should no longer rise in the morning because the light makes me sleep less. There's no way to stay asleep for what is coming. A few years ago I wrote a post, "10 Reasons You Have to Quit Your Job". The post had millions of views across many platforms. Many people liked that post because many people feel they are both unhappy in their jobs AND there is something better for them. People write me, 'I know I can fulfill my one true purpose if I only knew what it was."

"Choose Yourself!" which, along with its companion, *"The Choose Yourself Guide to Wealth"* contained most of the solution.

A container of water can't handle more water if it's already full of dirty water. That's how I was when I was at my lowest. Dirty, scummy, water. Nobody would drink it. Nobody would have me. I had to empty the container. I was getting a divorce and broke and losing my family, and I was miserable. The only solution was to not be an employee or an entrepreneur but a hybrid, what I will call in this book, "The Rich Employee", which is a combination of both mindset, and having the correct tools to survive and thrive in this economy and at this time.

I've written before about what it takes to clear out the container, to start fresh and to begin building those skills. In this book, I provide more details about how critical it is to develop the mindset of "The Rich Employee" and how that mindset can be used to catapult one to success and well-being. Is that the same as "Choosing Yourself?" It's *in addition* to. You Choose Yourself when you realize the veil of illusion bombarding us every day from every corner of society that seeks to control us under the guise that it wants to help us. People will laugh, fight, and ultimately, because there is no other choice, respect and reward the people who Choose Themselves.

THE BASICS:

Every day focus on 1% improvement of what I call "The Daily Practice".

PHYSICAL HEALTH:

Which, as my friend Tom Rath writes in "Are you Fully Charged?" comes down to "eat move sleep". Eat better. Move better. Sleep better. It doesn't mean: "Eat perfectly." It just means, eat this week a tiny bit better than you ate last week. As Tom put its, "We all know what's good for us and what's bad for us. Look at your plate and just make sure the positives outweigh the negatives. And do this for sleeping (8 hours is better than 2 hours) and for moving. Moving has become particularly important in our society: every trend has increased the amount of hours we sleep each week compared with our parents. More sedentary jobs, more sedentary sources of entertainment. Even the architecture of workplaces encourages sitting and little movement. This doesn't mean you have to drive to the gym and work out every day. As Nassim Taleb mentioned to me on our podcast, "many people drive two miles to the gym in order to walk two miles on a treadmill." Just walk. Walk a little more today than yesterday. And so on.

EMOTIONAL HEALTH:

Avoid spending time with people who bring you down. Spend more time with people you love and who love you. This doesn't mean run from the people you don't like. You can still open your heart to them. But you don't have to serve them dinner and champagne every night.

MENTAL HEALTH:

Exercise "The idea muscle" as discussed in all my books plus Claudia's "*Become an Idea Machine — Because Ideas are the Currency of the 21st Century*". This one thing has changed my life considerably every six months.

SPIRITUAL HEALTH:

Again, no extremes. This doesn't mean pray or meditate eight hours a day. It simply means "Gratitude". How often can you practice it per day? Maybe today a little more than yesterday? And so on. When I first wrote something similar to the above paragraph a woman wrote me back that "gratitude" and "emotional pain" cannot fit in her head at the same time. And that's exactly the idea. We only have a limited amount of time here on this tiny spaceship hurtling through the galaxy. Why waste a moment of it with pain. Now, I have a lot of pain often, enough to know that I choose what to do with it: I can stop for a second, notice it, and try to replace those regrets or anxieties with gratitude. Imagine our bodies as big blocks of stone. As Michelangelo said, every block of stone has a statue inside of it.

The Daily Practice is how we take the stone of ourselves, all of the places where we feel blocked, and turn those stones into works of art. In fact, it's really four stones: physical, emotional, mental, and spiritual, and the four works of art that we slowly begin to carve out become our own private museum. The way we dive deeper into ourselves and suddenly we see the art and poetry inside and it becomes breathtaking. We say, "I never knew I had that inside of me". I never knew I had those passions. I never knew I had that strength. I never knew I had those talents and the ability to say "yes" to the right things and "no" to the wrong things.

This is the first phase of Choosing Ourselves, when from the inside we find the beauty, we find the light that can shine across everything else, giving vision to others. The next phase is when we recognize the gatekeepers for what they are. The manager or bosses who could, with just the phrase: "You're fired", cause us so much emotional hurt and financial anguish.

Or the gatekeepers that would block our books from being published, or would say no to buying from us just when we needed that one last sale. Or the gatekeepers who would never acknowledge our art and our passions and force us to work in the figurative factories so we pay down the immense debts we accumulated because we thought they were the "dues" that society demanded from us (mortgages, student loan debt, etc.).

This second phase is the inauguration into the Idea Economy.

We now know that manufacturing and industry can be outsourced or duplicated. We now know that computers have largely replaced middle management. We are figuring out, as a society, that even knowledge can be outsourced. Right now I am outsourcing several programming projects to people in different countries, one translation project, several research projects, and several design projects. These are skills that are no longer needed in the most developed economies.

But one thing that can't be outsourced is Ideas. We are now transforming for the first time into a pure "Idea Economy". As I mention in "*The Choose Yourself Guide to Wealth*", ideas are the true currency of the 21st Century. Nothing can replace your ability to innovate, have a vision, and then execute on that vision in the most efficient way possible.

Many people have assumed that "Choosing Yourself!" automatically means becoming an entrepreneur.

This is completely not true. Entrepreneurship, of course, can be very lucrative. We see stories every day of people who start a company and then sell it a year later to Facebook or Google for billions. The heroes in our society have become the Mark Zuckerbergs or Elon Musks who seemed to pluck innovation from the sky and bring it to reality in their companies and make billions of dollars and help billions of people while they were at it. Because of decreasing incomes and less financial stability in the workplace people think they HAVE to become an entrepreneur to succeed and to find wellbeing in their lives.

This is not true. This book is about why it's not true and how you can obtain the Rich Employee mindset and enjoy the success earned by the few (and right now, its only a few) others who have this mindset and the skill set that comes with it. The problem is: income inequality is getting greater. There is no denying that. But this is not a distinction between Owner / Employee. This is a distinction between those with the Rich Employee mindset versus those with the Poor Employee mindset.

I have been an employee and an entrepreneur many times. There are good things and bad things about both. I've had wonderful experiences as an employee that allowed me to fulfill dreams, make money both at the job and on the side, and have the freedom to make any number of choices in my life. I've also had employee experiences where I couldn't wait to get "caught" doing a bad job so I could leave with severance and look for other opportunities.

I've experienced far greater volatility in my entrepreneur experiences. Don't forget that entrepreneurship is just like having a job with an 85% rate of failure. There is no way to predict or avoid that failure rate. Once you jump into that pool, it's too dark to see if a shark is waiting to eat you. But there's an 85% chance that a shark is there. It's scary and I've been bitten and torn to shreds by it. I'm not saying don't be an entrepreneur, by the way. But the average multi-millionaire has 14 different sources of income.

The goal of the entrepreneur in an Idea Economy is to not create risk for yourself and investors, but to mitigate that risk. Part of mitigating that risk is to choose yourself and fully participate in the Idea Economy whether you are an employee or an entrepreneur. Just like there are good entrepreneur opportunities, there are many opportunities to find the right companies where you can be an Entre-ployee. Meaning companies where participating in the Idea Economy will allow you to succeed and become wealthy right there on the job instead of thrashing in the startup slaughterhouse.

I've had to do this many times in order to survive. When you are entrepreneurial in the job, that could mean several things: You become so indispensable that your financial success gets immediately tied to the success of your efforts at the company.

You have side jobs, even entire side companies going on and everyone is fine with it (this is, in fact, how I started my first business, I stayed at the fulltime job for 18 months while building my initial business). You build more and more sources of income on the side so that your "job" is just another source of income for you. This book shows you how.

People might say: "But I don't have time to do a job AND a side gig". Yes you do. Don't worry about that now.

Entrepreneurship is a catchall phrase for starting your own company. Employee is a catchall phrase for working for someone else.

But there is a spectrum. If you are entrepreneurial at work and have the Rich Employee mindset then you get the best of both worlds. The supposed safety of a job has clearly become a myth, but the Entre-ployee has gotten rid of much of the risk of being fired. Or being tied to a bi-monthly paycheck that doesn't truly reflect the value you are bringing to the company — whether it's your own company, or someone else's, or a company you are building your own ownership in, bit by bit.

Since I've started applying these techniques and writing about them I have not looked back. And I've gotten hundreds of testimonials as to their success. Before I had a "Rich Employee" mindset I was struggling. I was afraid of my boss. I was afraid of my colleagues. I was afraid of what was going on in the economy because I had no real buffer if things fell apart, as they inevitably do. I remember lying in a hammock as I realized I was going to have to yet again sell my house and I had no idea what I would do for money. It was raining but I was afraid to go into the house and pretend to be on good behavior so I could be with my family. I don't think I made the decision then to become the Rich Employee. In fact, much failure happened after that moment. I did lose everything and my life became a living hell up until the point where I considered suicide after many nights of no sleep and my brain just battling me with every thought. Finally, I gave up. Why fight anymore. Just this moment, get healthy.

Nothing changed for that moment. But I felt like a weight lifted off of my shoulders. And little by little I developed these principles, many of which had worked for me in the past but I had forgotten about. Many of which I learned along the way. Every day I keep applying them. And it's not like every day is better than the last. It's still just like every day, but I find a bit more art inside the stone block that was given to me. And that's worth living for.

START THE ROAD TOWARDS
BECOMING A RICH EMPLOYEE
EXACTLY WHERE YOU ARE

············· ✳ ·············

I f this book caught your attention congratulations, you are in the right place. You are either at a job you don't like, or you were just fired. Maybe you are not sure if you should quit or start a business. Money and its creation can be confusing. Many of us have been all over the spectrum at one point or another, that is OK. Wherever you are, this is a great place to start.

We will start with the three more obvious places of what a rich employee would do if she was hired today, if he was fired today, and why he or she may need to stay at a job that sucks just for a while, until the full rich employee mentality kicks in. Let's get started.

10 THINGS A RICH EMPLOYEE DOES IF SHE OR HE HAS JUST BEEN FIRED

·············· ✳ ··············

That worst feeling is when you are suddenly called into a conference room and the only people there are your boss and the person from human resources whom you only met once before, on your first day on the job.

When it happened to me my brain didn't understand it ("what the...") but my heart was already splattered everywhere. I knew.

They told me I had to either take a 50% pay cut or I would be fired. If by chance I were fired they would give me severance. I didn't like either choice. I had responsibilities. I was counting on the money. I was scared. I wasn't expecting this. HR said: "I have to legally tell you this is the final decision." I was scared to go home. Not because of that sour taste of the next day already on my tongue but the stark fear of what I would be thinking when I would wake up in the middle of the night.

I knew I would wake up in the middle of the night feeling scared and lonely and insecure. Why would they want to fire me? I knew I would wake up paranoid and terrified.

I had one month to make a decision. So I did my thing and made a move in typical: "James-style"!

I did not make a decision. I did not show up for work at all in that month. I heard just the other day that everyone hated me at that job because they thought I was too arrogant to show up.

At the end of the month they told me I was fired but I was no longer entitled to the severance because I had let the month go by. They waited 32 days to tell me that last part. The severance would have been enough to keep me alive for six more months.

Now I was dead. I called up HR. I called the CEO. I called my friends there. I was crying while talking to the operator. It turned out I no longer had any friends. And the CEO's secretary said he would have to call me right back but he never did. There was nothing I could do. I had been stupid, fired, and now almost broke.

Again.

I hate being fired. And I hate hating being fired. It's like I'm begging someone who despises me to please enslave me one more time. Please! Just let me grovel and then you can fire me again and again at your slightest whim. I'll even take the 50% cut I'll take whatever you think a dog deserves. I'll even work for free! I said that to them. I needed money. I needed it fast. I had two choices: to panic or to take action.

When you panic, you live in your head. You sit there and go over and over and over again all the possible ways you're going to die. But you can't move. You always have two choices: to panic or to act with calm. Once a day I left my room and went to a gourmet hot dog place. I had a hot dog and then went back home and looked out the window for the rest of the day. I was frozen. Panic freezes you. Nobody is going to go into your head and take the panic away. But action leaks the panic out of your head.

I don't want to give advice. I just want to tell you what actions I took.

Another time I ran a company that was acquired. The new owners wanted me to fire people. I refused. Eventually they fired me. "You disgust me," said one of the people in charge.

I couldn't fire people, I didn't have the heart. "You have to do it," said my new boss. "If anything, this is the one situation where slavery is still enforced and you have to do what I say." That same guy is a famous movie producer now. One of his movies grossed over $300,000,000. So that was the end of that job.

Nothing ever works out when you are at the whims of others. It doesn't matter if you are an entrepreneur or an employee. Once someone is bribing you to do something (a salary is a form of bribery if you are only doing the work for the money and not for the meaning) then you become a prisoner.

Anybody can be a prisoner. There are many people who would be happy to be your prison guard. Everyone wants a piece. Everyone wants a cut. They get their cut, and you get left to bleed. Recently, an entire company I knew went down the drain. I had many friends there. I didn't want them to panic. I didn't want them to feel that fear.

I'm writing this book, in part, because of that fear. I hope people read this and learn that even being an employee one can choose oneself AND also succeed and thrive.

10 THINGS A RICH EMPLOYEE WILL DO IF SHE IS HIRED TODAY

············· ✳ ·············

The woman walking right next to me was alive one second, then a taxi came up on the sidewalk of 42 Street between 6 and 7 Avenue, hit her and veered off and now the woman was lying in the street, blood everywhere. This happened on the first or second day of my work when I started at HBO. I tried to call 911 in the payphone (there were still payphones in August, 1994) and then I had to go. The woman was dead. And I had to go to work. I loved HBO like I would love a parent. I wanted them to approve of me. And kiss me as I went to sleep at night.

Before I got the job offer I watched HBO all day long. My friend Peter and I would watch HBO or MTV for 10 hours straight. I'd go over his house around 1pm in the afternoon and by 10pm we would look at each other and say: "What the hell did we just do". Everything from the "the Larry Sanders Show" on HBO to "Beavis & Butthead" on MTV. We couldn't stop. I loved the product. I wanted to work there.

Looking back I see that what I was I doing then was the first rule a rich employee follows when she wants to work at a certain place, I loved the product. The rest of the rules came to me later on, as I was slapped in the face by life again and again. I learned the hard way. The good thing is you don't have to; here are the ten rules, all formulated and ready for you to take advantage of:

RULE #1:

LOVE THE PRODUCT

You have to love the current output of the company. If you work at HBO, love the shows. Watch every single show. No excuses. If you work at WD-40, know every use of WD-40. Make up a few more that nobody ever thought of. If you work at Otis Elevators, understand all the algorithms for how it decides which floors to stop on and when. If you work at Goldman Sachs, read every book on their history, study every deal they've done, know Lloyd Blankfein's favorite hobbies and how he rose through the ranks. You have to love the product the way Derek Jeter loves playing baseball.

When I started at HBO I would borrow VHS tapes from their library every day. I watched every show going ten years back. In my spare time I'd stay late and watch TV. I'd watch all the comedians. I even watched the boxing matches that initially made HBO famous. Which leads me to…

RULE #2:

KNOW THE HISTORY

At HBO, I learned how Michael Fuchs (the head of HBO Sports at the time. Later CEO of HBO) in 1975 aired the first boxing match that went out on satellite. And how Jerry Levin (the CEO of HBO, later CEO of Time Warner) used satellites to send the signal out to the cable providers. The first time that had ever happened. Ted Turner had been so inspired by that he turned his local TV affiliate, TBS, into a national TV station, and the rest became history.

RULE #3:

KNOW THE HISTORY OF
THE EXECUTIVES

At HBO I studied the org chart religiously. My title was "programmer analyst, IT department" and yet I was always asking around: how did John Billock become head of Marketing (he trudged around house to house selling HBO subscriptions in Louisiana when Showtime started up, for instance, decades earlier). Where did my boss's boss's boss's boss work before arriving at HBO? (Pepsi). Where did the head of Original Programming get his start? (He was a standup comedian, later CEO of HBO, before being forced to quit when choking his girlfriend in a Las Vegas parking lot). It was like reading about the origins of all the superheroes. I was a fan boy and my heroes were the other executives. I wanted to be one of them. Or better.

Same thing: know all of your colleagues and what their dreams and ambitions are. Get to work 2 hours before they get to work. If they need favors, do them. You have a whole two hours extra a day. You can do anything.

RULE #4:
MAKE YOUR BOSS LOOK GOOD

Your entire job in life is to make your boss look good. You don't care about yourself. You only want your boss to get promotions, raises, bonuses, etc. Remember that you can never make more than your boss. So the more he makes, the better he does, the better you will do. It's the only way to rise up. Work hard, give him full credit for everything you do. Don't take an ounce of credit. At the end of the day, everyone knows where credit belongs. But even then, thank him for everything and direct all credit back to him (or her). Here's how you make your boss look good:

Get to work two hours before him or her. If that means you have to wake up and go in at 5am then do it. Two extra hours of work a day is an extra 500 hours of work a year. None of your co-workers can compete with that. Walk with him to his car, or train when he leaves work. You need to know his goals, his initiatives, his plans, his family troubles, etc. And, again, give him full credit for everything. And thank him regularly for the opportunity to do the work you are doing.

RULE #5:

KNOW ALL THE SECRETARIES.

It's a cliché but the secretaries run the company. They control all of the schedules. They dish out all of the favors. Take as many secretaries out to lunch as possible. Not just in your department but in every department.

Pay particular attention to Human Resources, or the "People Department" because they know all of the gossip. They know everything that is happening. It's not so hard to do this. First off, HR gives you all of your intro material when you join the company. Ask those people out to lunch after you've settled in for a few weeks. If someone writes an internal company newsletter, ask that person to lunch. Ask your boss's boss's boss's boss's secretary out to lunch. Nobody will think you are going over his or her head. You're asking to lunch "just" a secretary. This was invaluable to me at every company I've ever worked at.

RULE #6:

TEST YOUR VALUE

Constantly test your value on the market. The job market is like any other market. There's supply and demand. And you're just an item for sale at the great bazaar. Every year you need to find out what your value is on the market. For one thing, the best way to get an increase in salary and status is to move horizontally, not vertically.

Second, you don't want to get inbred. A good friend of mine was in HBO's marketing department for 17 years. I set up a dinner inviting her, the CEO of an advertising agency that was hiring, and me. The CEO was one of my closest friends. Still, she couldn't hire my HBO friend. "She's too inbred," she said. "She will never be able to get the HBO way of doing things out of her head."

When I was at HBO I was constantly talking to people at other companies. I had lunch with top people at Showtime. I knew people from all the other divisions of Time Warner. I was always asking people to lunch or breakfast. I would get offers from the banking industry. I would try to work within different divisions of HBO. Every time I got another offer, I got another raise and promotion at HBO, sometimes substantial (up to 35% increase). My bosses would resent me for it, but then going back to "Rule #4", often they would get raises as well.

By the way, I am very shy. If I go to a party, I'm the one standing in the corner with nothing to say.

I think many people are introverted. But the secret is: introverts have a very powerful skill. They can listen. It doesn't take a lot to ask a person to lunch. You send an email.

And then you listen. Soon, you will have listened to everyone. And they are all happy to talk to you. You will know their problems. You will know how you can help them, and you will. That's how you become indispensable.

Rule #7:

Study the Marketing Campaigns

Study all the marketing campaigns. For example, in 1996 HBO switched their slogan to "It's not TV. It's HBO". That slogan lasted for 13 years. Before that it was "Simply the Best", then "Something Special's On". When they switched to "It's not TV", Eric Kessler, the head of marketing, gave a talk on how they came up with the slogan. All his employees were in the auditorium. And me, from the IT department. Nobody else would go with me. I knew every slogan HBO ever had.

Rule #8:

Study the Industry

What made HBO different from Showtime, or from Cinemax? Or from non-pay cable? Or broadcasting? I read every book about the history of TV I could find. I would go to lectures at the Museum of Radio and Television on 52 Street. The best was a day that members of the MTV show "The Real World" gave a panel. After the panel I followed one group of other people in the audience for 30 blocks while they talked about the panel and the show. I wanted to break in so many times. They would be my new best friends. We would have parties around showings of "The Real World". But I was too shy and eventually they all split off in different directions, leaving me alone. Jessica Reif Cohen was the Merrill analyst covering media. I knew nothing about stocks. But I read everything she wrote and would scan the WSJ for mentions of her name.

When I was trying to sell my first company, Reset. I called every company in the industry. Omnicom, Razorfish, Agency.com, etc. I read every SEC filing so I would know the nuances of all their deals and financings. When I was building Stockpickr I became obsessed with the mechanics of how Yahoo Finance worked and the ways in which she (Yahoo Finance is a "she", and I love her) delivered traffic to all of her media sources. With HBO it was fascinating because at one point the CEOs of Showtime, Time Warner, Universal, Viacom, Fox Sports, etc. were all former executives of HBO.

RULE #9:

BECOME THE COMPANY

I was a lowly programmer in the IT department. We were so far from the normal business operations of the company that they even put us in a different building. But that didn't matter to me. I *was* HBO. That was my mantra. I became so absorbed in every aspect of the operations that I knew any idea I had would be a good idea for the company. At least I felt this (not sure if anyone else did). I never said, "I think this", I said, "We should do this". HBO and I were a "We". Inseparable.

Until you have that feeling of unity with the company you work for, you can't rise up. Key, though: when you have an idea, make sure you know how to execute the idea also, and in detail. Clear guides for execution is worth a million dollars. And I mean that specifically, if you execute on a good idea, you'll make a million dollars or more from it.

RULE #10:

LEAVE

All good things must come to an end. From the day you start, you need to plan your exit. Not like in rule #6, "Know Your Value" where you are trying to figure out your corporate salary value. *Leave* means something different.

It means you're going to say goodbye forever. If you master Rules #1-9 at a company then you'll know enough about the company and industry to start your own company. To either become a competitor or a service provider. And you will have built in customers because your list of contacts and your extended network will be filled with people from the industry. If you constantly think like an entrepreneur from the instant you walk into your cubicle on day one of your job then you will be constantly looking for those missing gaps you can fill. This is how you jump into the abyss. You make sure the abyss has a customer waiting for you.

I did everything wrong in my first few months at HBO. I didn't know NYC. I didn't know corporate culture at all. I wore the same suit five days in a row until I realized nobody else was wearing a suit and I never wore one again. I didn't have the requisite skill set to survive at my job (they had to send me to a remedial programming school despite the fact that I had majored in programming AND went to graduate school for computer science). I was obsessed with the Internet and HBO didn't even own HBO.com at the time. My boss's boss's boss would say to my boss, "get him away from that Internet stuff and onto some real work."

One time my boss came into my cubicle and with everyone listening from every other cubicle said to me, "we want you to succeed here but you need to know more or else it's not going to work out." It was very embarrassing and nobody around me would meet my eyes for the next week or so. I was the walking dead. I was sure I was going to get fired every day.

But I survived then. And every day since.

10 Reasons A Rich Employee Will Stay At Her or His Job: For NOW...

················ ✳ ···············

I used to love my job. Love it. I worked for my favorite entertainment company in the world.

I would've paid to work there. I made friends at work. And on weekends we'd even get together and play poker. Sometimes we'd even travel on vacations together. My boss would yell at me but I could ignore him. So I forgive you. I loved the work I was doing. What could be better than being paid to interview prostitutes and drug dealers at three in the morning in the sleaziest most dangerous parts of New York City. I was chased once with a knife. I once had a bottle thrown at me. I had guards at transvestite clubs chase me. And I had a lot of fun! All for money.

I will tell you what is better than that, because I can't be so arrogant to think that nothing is better than that. Walking on the moon is better than that. And maybe being a clown in a large circus. Or a famous street magician. But not much else. I always write about "ten reasons to quit your job". Of course I still believe that. You should quit your job.

But maybe *not today*.

Not everything is black and white. For instance, when I day traded for a living, many years later, there were some days when I would go to work and LOSE money. WOAH!

Sometimes in the morning I was so afraid to lose more money I'd go to the Catholic Church across the street and pray to Jesus that Nasdaq futures would go up in the morning. I'm Jewish so it never worked. That never happens at a job. At a job you go into work and they send you a check every two weeks. That's real magic. A lot of times people think the alternative to a job is to be an entrepreneur. That's not true either. An entrepreneur is someone who *has* a job, but it's a job he made up all by herself. She woke up one day and said, "I'm going to make an app to connect all left-handed people on a dating site." And then she raised money, hired people, made an app, tried to sell the app.

An entrepreneur has a job also. But here's the difference. In a regular job you can probably get by (maybe unhappily but still get by) forever. But an entrepreneur has a very high chance of failure. Which would you rather take? I don't want people to stay at a job. There are several good things about having a job. We can't ignore them. Here's a few things to think about it. And I finish with the alternative.

A) STEADY PAYCHECK

It might go down over time and you might get fired suddenly but for a while, at least, it's steady.

B) FRIENDSHIP

The friendships don't always last. Once you leave the job you may never see them again. You might not even really like them. But while you are at the job, there's always opportunities to learn from the people around you. And the more you help the people around you and find meaning in the work that *they* do, the more satisfied you will be at your own job. And the more indispensable you will become.

C) CHANCE OF PROMOTION

I don't know if promotion is good or bad. But for about a day or two you think, "they like me! They really like me!"

D) FAKE MONEY

If you rise really high at your job then it's as if the entire company is your fake bank account. They pay for your travel, your computers, many of your dinners. They might even pay for some of your friends.

E) RESPECT!

If you become the CEO of your job then people will respect you. It's not easy to be the CEO of a big company. I'll tell you what you have to do to be CEO of a big company:

- You have to work in many divisions of the company so you know what they all do.
- You have to build relationships with the other board members of the company so when the time is right they pick you.
- Go on vacations with the biggest customers so you become indispensable. It's not such a bad thing to go on vacations.
- Build connections between the different divisions. Always be the behind the scenes guy. You know what happens after that? Behind the scenes becomes in front of the scenes and you are the CEO.
- Make a lot of money for the company. This seems hard. But it just involves signing one or two large customers or large distribution partners or launching a lot of products, one of which might become successful. Try things long enough and you will make a lot of money for your company.

- Always over-promise and over-deliver. Sometimes people hate that. They want to under promise and over deliver. *Don't do that.* That's stupid! Most jobs are not so hard to over-promise at because for years, the employees before you have been under-promising. And the jobs are not that hard. What... Are you trying to launch a spaceship to the Moon? Overpromise and over deliver and you will keep getting promoted because nobody else is doing it.

F) You Can Afford to Have an Evil Plan

When I had a job I started a company on the side. I was also trying to pitch TV shows. I was doing lots of things on the side. I was a hustler. My bosses didn't mind because I was overpromising and over delivering. I started a company in 1996. My new company took me eight hours a day at least. But it wasn't until August, 1997 that I left my fulltime job to join my new company. As I said before, it took 18 months.

Why did it take so long?

Because that is how life works. You don't start something and suddenly everything changes. You start something, make sure it's right, test the waters, build up, get rid of all the risks, and then make the jump.

Being an entrepreneur is NOT about taking risk, it's about ELIMINATING all risk. Being an entrepreneur, or having multiple sources of income is ultimately safer than having a job, but only if you use the job to get rid of all the risks. Just being an entrepreneur, without having multiple sources of income, without first taking care of the risks, is suicide.

G) BE AN ENTRE-PLOYEE

Maybe you like the people you work with and you like what you are doing. I wish I were you. At a job you can do something that you can't do elsewhere. You can *link* your financial success (or other kinds of success) to the success of the larger company. If you can figure out how to do this, then you can stay at your job forever and watch it grow. If you can't figure out how to do this then you MUST QUIT.

But only after eliminating risks.

I was always trying to figure out how to convince HBO to spin off new divisions or companies that maybe I could help run. It never worked out. Nobody listened to me. But I tried. A great example is the world famous Craig Silverstein. Oh wait! You don't know him? He's a low-level programmer at the Khan Academy. But before that he was the first employee ever at Google. And now he's a billionaire. His success was totally tied to the success of Google. Google is a search engine on the world-wide-web.

H) SUMMERS ARE OFF

The first summer I was at a full time job it was really heaven. Most of management basically took off the summer. Deadlines on all of our projects slowed down. My office was right by a park so I'd sit in the park all day and play chess.

When you're an entrepreneur you don't have summers off. You don't even have three in the morning off. I'd wake up at three in the morning and try to calculate out how I was going to make payroll for the next six months. It was really painful.

1) You Get to Switch Jobs

The average American employee stays at their job for 3 years. This number is getting smaller and smaller. People move around jobs. Get lots of experiences. Meet lots of people. Make more and more money (hopefully). And then, when they have enough contacts and experiences they can set themselves up in a situations where they have multiple streams of income. Maybe this means they start doing speaking gigs. Based on all of their work experiences and knowledge in an industry. Maybe it means they consult. Maybe it means they learn new skills and now start using those skills to help other people. Because if they have a steady paycheck they can build these side gigs over time and eventually start charging. That's what I did, *twice*. That's what I would do today.

Don't jump over the cliff. Have ropes and safety gear.

It doesn't mean start "a company". Then you are just going from one company to another. Rather, start generating a lot more money from many different sources and if any one source is cut off then it's not the end of the world. It's just an opportunity to replace that one source of money with an even bigger source.

And maybe I know what you are thinking…

I write a lot about reasons to quit your job. I write a lot about how life can be better elsewhere. But life is always better elsewhere. We're nomadic mammals. Also, many jobs are bad. The worst thing about a job is your boss. Then your co-workers., then your pay, then your work. Then the fact that one person can say words that turn your life upside down: "you're fired". So get yourself in a situation with more of the attributes I describe in the ten reasons above. Then it's up to *you* to decide the right time to quit. It's no longer up to a mysterious "Them".

The important thing to remember is this:

Jobs, as our parents knew it, are dead. Income has gone down versus inflation for 40 years. People are being demoted and spending fewer years at a job:

- VIEW A JOB AS JUST ONE SOURCE OF INCOME AMONG MANY.
- BUILD UP YOUR SOURCES OF INCOME.
- BE CREATIVE.
- WRITE A BLOG.
- DO CONSULTING ON THE SIDE.
- GET MORE SKILLS.
- DO SPEAKING.
- BE AN ENTRE-PLOYEE.

Then suddenly you won't have "just" a job. You wont' be an entrepreneur. You won't have any label attached to your money. Have your evil plan. Do it in secret. Work on it a little bit each day. 1% a day. Stay calm. Don't be impatient or entitled.

Then you'll be your own person. Nobody will be your boss. There won't be a ceiling when it's finally time to spread your wings and fly into the sky.

WHY BE A RICH EMPLOYEE?

WHY YOU MUST URGENTLY BECOME A RICH EMPLOYEE, RIGHT NOW

· · · · · · · · · · · · · · ✳ · · · · · · · · · · · · · · ·

A lot of angry people out there are trying to control you and even kill you. I bet you can list at least a dozen people trying to control you right now. I wrote an article on my email list the other day saying how I was paid up on my taxes for the first time ever but that it made me sick to my stomach.

Taxes and money are very emotional issues for many people. Some people wrote me angry letters. In two cases I wrote back: "Please reread the article" and then they reread and apologized. How come they apologized? Because they didn't read it. They just projected their own anger onto my article and then onto me. That's what most people do all of the time. They are sick but they puke on you. They wanted to provoke a response from me. They wanted to control me.

I have two challenges: not letting people control me, and not trying to control anyone else. When I succeed at these two things, life is pretty good. The first time I ever made a lot of money it did not make me free. It cost me my freedom. Before I had money I had a lot of friends, I did what I wanted on weekends and at nights, I had fun. After I had money I started thinking I needed to make more money, a LOT more money. I started buying things I couldn't afford. I felt people wouldn't like me if I didn't have these things. I started lending money out to friends and family in the hopes of "helping" them. I thought people would like me if I "saved" them.

Nobody will ever remember how you helped them. And you cannot save anyone. This was my first lesson.

My second lesson is that I never really owned anything. When I "owned" a house I became a slave to the bank, a slave to the government, a slave to up-keeping the house, a slave to the other people living in the house (my family, who I became afraid would be homeless).

Third, I let money control who I associated with. Eventually I ended up with no friends or family. The people I truly loved at the time, I lost. I still regret it. I was afraid of consequences. I was afraid to lose "everything" even though I had already lost it. I sold everything. I had to give up many of my friendships and even many of my family relationships. I disappointed probably everyone. But it was the only way I could get free and start from scratch. Once I started from scratch I was able to begin the long process of reinventing myself. I own next to nothing right now except some clothes and some books. And all my relationships, 100% of the people I talk with, are only with people I choose to talk to.

If someone in my life tries to control me because of their own fears and angers, then they are out. I also try not to control anyone else. If someone does something I don't like, I can't control what they may think or do. It's useless and it's a waste of my time. I try to change my circumstances so I don't have to deal with those people.

What if you are stuck in a job and have bills to pay because of past mistakes? You have to work for your freedom then. And it's an ongoing process. It's every day. The key to freedom is Luck. But luck is not magic.

Luck equals 1) — Persistence, plus 2) — Diversification.

1 . Persistence is a sentence filled with failures punctuated by the occasional success.

2 . Diversification means coming up with thousands of ideas and implementing the one or two percent that seem reasonable.

Coming up with 1000s of ideas means having the energy and creativity to brainstorm. Energy equals Physical plus Emotional plus Mental plus Spiritual health. All forms of health are a function of how much you control your own life divided by how many people control you. When I respond to an angry comment, someone controls me. Anger controls me. Then I spend less time being healthy.

If I'm in an unhappy relationship but afraid of the consequences of breaking it then fear controls me. If I daydream arguments between myself and a boss or a sister or a colleague or whoever, then anger is controlling me. Their issues have nothing to do with me. If I let them control me, or I try to control them I sacrifice my health. Then I can't generate ideas. I lose persistence. I get unlucky. I lose my freedom. Every time. No exceptions. I'd much rather be healthy than "right".

Many people have written about things like "the law of attraction". The law of attraction is about attracting things in the outside world into your life. This is fine. But it won't work unless you control what's happening on the inside world first. Unless you can embrace and face the mess of your own emotional makeup. Unless you can stop believing every thought your mind keeps repeating in an infinite loop. This is the one thing truly under your control. The ability to ignore the instant chatter of the mind and to recognize there is something beyond it. There is wisdom beyond it, from the fountain of silence. This is the only way to choose yourself. This book is committed to giving you the tools that work in this century, in this time and age, and in this new world, post 2008.

Don't be the slave. Be the master.

How to Be a 'Master' Or At Least: The Smartest 'Rich Employee' In The Room

· · · · · · · · · · · · · · · ✳ · · · · · · · · · · · · · ·

I was the dumbest person in my graduate school program, which is part of the reason I was thrown out. Stupidity plus immaturity and a willingness to show off both qualities is a bad combination. I thought I was a cowboy. I would show up to final exams having not attended a single class, totally smashed from the night before and not having slept. I had semesters where I failed every single class. I did everything you could possibly do to piss off as many people as possible in as short amount of time as possible and eventually I got thrown out. Well, I was "asked" to leave. I'm not defending myself. I took bad advantage of a great situation I was in. They paid me a stipend and I used it to do whatever I wanted to.

Later, when I moved to the corporate world I was the stupidest person there as well. Probably because I failed to learn anything in graduate school. I got the job for various reasons that had nothing to do with my abilities and so they didn't know what to do with me. I was so impressed with everyone running around, knowing what to do, and knowing how to survive in the big city. I thought to myself, "these are the real people and I'm faking it." On my second day they gave me a computer to put on the Internet. They said: "You know something about that internet stuff. Get this thing on the Internet. But be careful, we keep some email servers on this." I destroyed that computer so badly it had to be sent back to the manufacturer (Silicon Graphics) and it never came back. I was wearing a suit that didn't fit me. I never wore suits. It was sunny out. I went outside to use the payphone.

No sense making a call like this from my cubicle. I called my girlfriend in Pittsburgh and told her I was about to be fired. She was pretty happy about that. She wanted me back. Which unfortunately, was my worst nightmare.

Jolie Hunt at Reuters invited me to a dinner a last year. I was definitely 100 IQ points lower than anyone there. Tina Brown was sitting next to me. Shawkut Azziz, the former prime minister of Pakistan was across from me. Padma Lakshmi was next to him. I don't even know why I was invited. I concluded during the dinner that I must've done a favor at some point for Jolie but I couldn't remember what it was. The list goes on of the people at this dinner. Everyone had something to say. One of my favorite authors, Ken Auletta, was drilling the former prime minister about how much Pakistan knew about Osama Bin Laden's whereabouts. I was deathly afraid someone would look at me and say: "Well, what do you think about all of this? What do you have to say for yourself?"

But after 40+ years of being the least smart person in most situations that I've been put in I've finally figured out how to be the smartest person on the planet.

The key: *always* assume you are the *least* intelligent person in the room. Always. Do this in every room, at every dinner, in every situation.

Several things will happen:

A) YOU'LL LISTEN AND LEARN FROM EVERYONE AROUND YOU:

They are all smarter than you. Which means you have a lot to learn from them. Sergey Brin has a trick when he interviews people for Google. He can tell within seconds whether or not he is going to hire someone. If he's not going to hire them he knows he still has to suffer through another twenty minutes with them. So he always makes it a point to learn at least one thing from them so it's not a total waste of time. I do this with every person I meet ever. Because I happen to know a secret about them: they are smarter than me.

This is not a false humility. I haven't been very good at school (which is probably why I write so many articles about why college is bad). And I haven't made a billion dollars despite the opportunities I've had. I've made many stupid mistakes that I have a hard time forgiving myself for. I could've saved lives and instead I squandered them. I got good at squandering.

The good thing I have going for me is that I LOOK smart. I have curly hair and glasses. And I'm Jewish and people stereotype all of the above. Oh, and I'm good at chess. Which people also equate with intelligence but this isn't true.

B) When you're done listening, listen to the silence:

Trust me, people never finish talking. Once you've learned something from someone and they are done talking, then skip your turn to talk and let them talk again. They'll do it. Not because of arrogance. It's because they have more to teach you. So listen some more.

C) Now when they are done talking, ask at least one question.

They'll do A and B again. You'll learn more. As I'm writing this it almost feels like I'm making fun of the people I'm listening to. But that couldn't be further from the truth. Every time I learn more.

D) INTELLIGENCE COMPOUNDS EXPONENTIALLY. IT'S THE "NETWORK EFFECT":

In a system (like the Internet) with the network effect, the more people that use it, the value of the entire network goes up exponentially. Which is why the value and profit of companies like Facebook have gone up so fast compared with companies in prior generations. And why the entire Internet exploded upwards like it did. But in the case of intelligence, the "network" is the neurons in your brain. Learn new things and new neurons wake up and start firing synapses with each other, increasing exponentially the "value" (intelligence) of the "network" (your brain).

So try this: be the least intelligent person at every meeting and gathering. You're a spy, gathering all the Intel you can. Unlike everyone else at the meeting, you are guaranteed to learn something (because everything people say is something you don't know, almost by definition). Because of the compounding effect, at some point, you will be the smartest.

E) HUMILITY:

At the very least, assuming you are smart, you will be able to practice and cultivate a healthy humility, which is never bad.

But, you might ask: shouldn't one exude confidence and demonstrate intelligence so people are impressed?

No! People will forget you. Not everyone, but most. Because that's what people do. They move onto the next thing. People will not remember what you said, they will remember how you made them feel, if you consciously cultivate humility and learn from everyone you meet, they will remember you. And, before long, you'll be the smartest person on the planet. And when the aliens land and say: "we are going to talk to your leader", everyone around you will be surprised when the aliens go straight to you.

THE RICH EMPLOYEE VERSUS
THE POOR EMPLOYEE MENTALITY:
HOW A RICH EMPLOYEE THINKS

·············· ✳ ··············

W hen Michael Eisner became CEO of Disney, the first thing
he did was walk through Disneyland, checking out his new
domain. While walking through the park he noticed some
garbage on the ground. He picked it up and threw it out. The CEO of the
company was, at that moment, the janitor of the company.

Why did he do that?

This is a loaded question. Obviously he wants the park to be clean in an ideal
world. But there are other things to ask here. Why did he even notice the
garbage? It was just a crumpled piece of paper. He noticed it because "good,
clean, fun" is part of the brand of Disney. People know they can bring their
kids there and it's going to be the same experience every time. They can rely
on that experience. They know when their child is born, that 5 years from
now they can bring their kid to Disneyland and it will basically be the same
experience they had when they were a kid. Not garbage all over the place,
not rotting equipment, or bad food. None of that, but rather: new rides,
smiling characters, and cleanliness.

Second, why did Michael Eisner pick up the garbage rather than yell at the
nearest janitor to clean up the garbage. Or pretend to ignore it and then later
send out an angry memo demanding that all garbage be picked up? Because
excellence spreads like a disease. It doesn't spread from the top down like

54

many people think (although that is ONE way it spreads). Michael Eisner knew that if people saw him take notice of, and take care of, the smallest detail involved in the protection of the brand, then their key to success within the company is to do the same. To notice, to execute, to improve for another day the values promoted by the company and the brand it conveys.

When Michael Eisner took over Disney, people were worried that the increase in entertainment choices (computer games, the Internet, etc.) would overwhelm people and cause park attendance to decrease. While he was there he certainly made mistakes. A good rule of thumb is to remember that in business, if only 51% of your decisions are good then you are probably doing an A+ job. But during his tenure at Disney, the stock price went up 1646%.

When Bob Iger took over as CEO, guess what was the first thing he did?

He walked through the park, saw a piece of garbage, broke away from the entourage following his every movement, and picked up a piece of garbage and threw it away. Since then the stock price of Disney is up 420%. Which is 1000% better than the increase in the overall stock market during the same time frame. Now, you can say, "these guys were the CEOs. What does this have to do with being an employee?"

The CEO is basically the lowest employee. He has the most bosses, the most constituencies to cater to. He has to cater to customers, investors, board members, employees, banks, and the media. Imagine if you weren't the CEO, but the CEO was passing by. You both see the garbage on the floor but he goes to pick it up and you keep walking. What if he notices that you kept walking?

At that point you basically have zero chance of being a rich employee.

Another way to look at it is what I mentioned earlier. Excellence ripples out and doesn't just come from the top down. When your colleagues see you performing above-and-beyond, without doing it front of a spotlight, with no seeming reward, then you set the bar for excellence in your group. Keep setting the bar in unexpected ways and suddenly you become the bar that everyone strives to be like. "Why should I do that if there's no reward?"

In every research study on excellence in the workplace it turns out that thinking about money reduces your ability to perform on the job. It even has been shown that if you are reminded about your salary right before a meeting, you'll sit on average 12 inches further from your co-employees.

Everything in life comes down to meaning. Victor Frankl writes about this so beautifully in his book, "Man's Search for Meaning" where he describes his own survival in concentration camps and attributes that survival to always finding meaning in what he was doing. In his case, he found meaning in finding his family again. And in the thought that eventually he would write about his experiences.

Am I comparing a job to Auschwitz? Of course not. But often in situations where we feel discouraged or "stuck" (as many people put it), the key is not to stay in our head, going over all the reasons we are in such a miserable place. The key is to actually get out of our head and find someone to encourage. Use the slogan: when discouraged, encourage others. This is how you get out of your head.

This is where trust comes in. And I am not talking about a mystical sort of trust, but rather a trust that excellence is noticed and rewarded in the long run. It might not be today. It might not be at this company. It might not be with this boss. But it is a habit that if you remain consistent with, you will be rewarded.

By the way, in our entire education, from first grade through last grade, we're taught that a 90% is an A. An 80% is a B. And so on.

But I just said that all a great CEO has to do is "get" a 50%. Well, in our standardized educational system, a 50% is an "F".

So we have to get over the instinct that getting 50% of our decisions correct constitute failure. In fact, that's a massive A+. So to be a good CEO, to be the "rich employee" means re-educating yourself on what success is. Often, this is very difficult once we hit the wall that is the real world. But it's one of the most important lessons to learn to be successful.

· · · · · ✳ · · · · ·

A Rich Employee Ties his Financial Success to the Financial Success of the Company

Craig Silverstein was the first employee of Google. He probably programmed much of the original search engine, which was based on Larry Page's PageRank algorithm. Arguably this is an extreme case. Craig is now a billionaire because of his efforts at Google. But it's worth pointing out, that he didn't start his own company. In fact, right now, billionaire that he is, he's an employee at another company — Khan Academy, the online education startup started by Sal Khan.

This is where he currently finds meaning. First, creating the best search engine in the Internet , he helped catalog all of the information in the world for the first time ever.

And now he finds meaning in changing the way society is educated.

There's something called "entre-pornography" out there (well, actually, I just made that up) where everyone goes on and on how great it is to be an entrepreneur.

It's not so great to be an entrepreneur. I've been many times both an entrepreneur and an employee. They are both basically the same if you have the philosophy and approach of "the rich employee".

Title doesn't matter. Salary doesn't matter. It's how you deliver value and create excellence around you that matters. Title and salary work themselves out over time. I went from Junior Programmer Analyst making $40,000 a year at HBO to being CEO of my own company and making millions to being dead broke within a 6 year time period. And I did that route more than once.

The problem with being an entrepreneur is it's like being an employee except for two things: YOU create the job with well-known percentage of failure (85%), and, almost by definition (else the percentage would be much lower) there is absolutely no way to predict the future. Nobody knew in advance that Alta-Vista, the world's best search engine in 1997, would fail and Google would succeed.

The only thing you have control over is your mindset, your habits, and the choices you make internally about how you're going to deal with a situation. Most of our life, the situation we have to deal with throughout the day is our job and our career. Do we let our job choices control us or do we control them by having the mindset of the rich employee? That's what this section is about, that's what this book is about.

When Craig Silverstein started working with his Stanford friends, Sergey Brin and Larry Page, he had no idea how it would turn out. He was their employee after they got their very initial programming. Someone had to program the search engine so he did it. As the company grew, he became director of technology. Often as a company gets bigger, the technology innovation starts to stagnate. Craig was aware of that and created what he called "grouplets" which allowed the programmers within the company to keep the feel of a small company as they worked on projects in small groups while still taking advantage of the resources of a now gigantic company.

Did he leave Google as soon he became a billionaire? Of course not. He was changing the world. That's worth a lot more than money. When he finally did leave Google did he become a billionaire philanthropist playboy? Of course not. He's now a "programmer" at the Khan Academy. He believes in charity, he said, but he was too young to quit working. So he became an employee for a company devoted to a cause he believes in: online education. And in doing so, he is able to provide his full resources behind the cause.

What do I mean by "full resources"? Craig's skills are simple: he's a programmer. That's what he was trained to do. But often we develop other more intangible skills along the way if we are going to deliver excellence wherever we work: leadership, an ability to inspire others, an ability to help define a vision, to execute on a vision, and so on. If Khan Academy ultimately delivers on its promise and has a multi-billion dollar exit, I'm sure Craig Silverstein will enormously benefit as well. And at the same time: he'll keep saving the world along the way.

· · · · · ✳ · · · · ·

A Rich Employee Over-Promises and Over-Delivers

I've been a manager many times in my career in at least four different industries. We live in an economy where often the way we meet our employees is first through assigning projects to freelancers. This happens for two reasons: Often I don't know what projects will really turn out to be worthwhile until they are already done and I can see them. But the second reason is: I often don't know whom to hire for a particular job. So often I will outsource to more than one person the exact same job. Then it's easy to see who is over delivering. Someone who comes back to me with a solution that blows my mind away. He or she didn't do simply what I asked, he taught me something new in my very own project. I want to hire the people who teach me, who when I ask for X, will deliver X + Y, where Y is above and beyond anything I could have thought of on my own.

I also like it when someone says: "I can do this. But how about we also X alongside" and I suddenly realize that X will increase the value of what I initially asked. How can I not hire that person? How can I not throw money at that person? How can I not want that person to succeed?

By the way, it doesn't matter if I want that person to succeed or not. He's *going to succeed*. So I better get behind that success so I can also benefit from it on that person's rise all the way to the top. I'm not the most successful person I know. But some of the most successful people I know used to work for me. Does this help me or hurt me? Don't I feel resentful? Of course not, because 100% of the time it helps me. That person might later buy a company I started. Or give me ideas I never thought of, or make introductions I could never had made on my own.

Are you ever in a situation where you say, "Wow, I can't believe I'm meeting so-and-so." Almost every time I am in one of those situations it's because it's either someone who is over delivering who made the introduction, or someone who totally surpassed me in his or her success who is now carrying me along with him. I don't mind being carried. It's relaxing.

· · · · · ✳ · · · · ·

A Rich Employee Gets to Work Early

Ok. Now we get to "no sleep" porn. I hate that guy who says, "I only need three hours of sleep". It's just not true. Every single study shows that people need sleep. And it makes sense. In the morning, the brain is relaxed and awake. And at night the brain is tired so needs sleep. Maybe there are one or two superhuman people who only need 3 hours of sleep. But the few that I have known have all been mentally ill. And I mean it. I have yet to meet someone who says, "I only need three hours of sleep," who isn't lying or who isn't mentally sick. The average concert violinist needs 8.6 hours of sleep for instance.

Lack of sleep is related to all sorts of troubles: heart trouble, diabetes, strokes, etc. Not only that, recent research shows that during sleep, any neurotransmitters or neurons that may need "regeneration" are healed while we sleep. Essentially, people who sleep 8 hours a day live longer, healthier, less stressful lives. So can we get to work early and still get the amount of sleep we need?

When I worked at HBO I would try to get to work by about 6am every morning. Most people would come in around 10am. This was amazing for me. I had four hours of uninterrupted work time. In other words, by the time everyone else was just starting to arrive at work, I had already accomplished more than what most of them would do during the day.

Let's say you work a 9-5 job. You get in at 9 and there's the usual gossip or whatever until 9:30. Maybe you have a meeting in the morning so that takes another chunk out of the day. Let's say it's now 10:30. Many employees take some sort of mid-morning break. Now it's 11. Lunch is at noon. So one hour of work got done. Then comes the hour of lunch. Then it's hard to be as mentally focused right after your eat which is why in many cultures the "siesta" is a mandatory part of the day. Counting in the mid-afternoon break and maybe another meeting, how many hours of work really happens in the typical workday?

According to Dan Ariely, the human brain is at its peak productivity about 2-5 hours after you wake up. So if you wake up at 5am then from 7-9 or 7-10am your brain is about 100x more productive than it is in the evening. If you wait until late afternoon or evening to get done with your critical work items, it will be much more difficult and will create worse results.

So getting in early is not about working all day and night. In fact, it's the opposite. It's about working when your brain is at it's peak. It's about being uninterrupted while you work. If you are working on anything that requires concentration or creativity then there are many studies that show a single interruption can force you to take up to 20 minutes to get back in "the zone" so you are at peak productivity again.

During 9-5 it's almost impossible to have that uninterrupted time. And if you get work done like this, it's easier to then spend the later parts of the day focusing on whatever meetings you have to attend, helping others get their work done, and maybe even leaving early if you feel like it. Why not? You need to get to spend time with friends and family and get to sleep early.

Some people might say, "I can't do this." Perhaps they have kids or too big of a commute, or any number of things. That's ok. Often there are still periods in the day you can find where you maybe skip the lunch and eat at your desk or don't let anyone disturb you for the first hour or so you are at your desk.

But, that said, there are also many solutions where you can hire a babysitter in the morning so you can get in work early. And then perhaps spend more time with your family later in the day.

· · · · · ❊ · · · · ·

A R I C H E M P L O Y E E — I S L O Y A L

Because he loves the values of the company, not because he is told to.

· · · · · ❊ · · · · ·

A R I C H E M P L O Y E E — D O E S N O T G O S S I P

Humans gossip for a reason. As a species we started off in small tribes, like any other mammal. Tribes bigger than 30 humans were often split into two and each tribe went their own way. Why is 30 such a special number? Because for most of us, it's possible to get to know 30 people well enough to know whether or not "this person has my back" about each person in the tribe. Above 30, it's often hard to know that. When companies grow above 30, it's often hard to know who are the reliable employees you can work with and who aren't. So what happens? How did humans learn to grow in bigger groups? In fact, it was our ability to work in larger tribes than 30 that many scientists theorize is the reason why we are the only "humans" left. Where did the Neanderthals go?

Gossip served the useful function that if I knew Claudia, but you didn't, I could say, "Don't worry. Claudia is good to work with. She's a great hunter with a knife." Now, because you trust me (a big "if") you can also trust Claudia even if you don't know her. That is why gossip became crucial to the survival of the human species and to any group setting larger than about 30. So why am I saying "Don't Gossip"? Because 200,000 years later, we're usually not worried about whom we are hunting and killing with. If we're in a group larger than 30 (and we always are) we often fill in the gaps of conversation with what our species naturally evolved to do: we gossip, even if it's not about hunting. So we might say, "Guess where Harry was last night?" and gossip begins. Guess what? Harry will find out. Because of this natural inclination to not keep secrets, people always find out. And when people find out, the result is painful.

I know of many people who were previously close friends who I have heard talk behind my back. How do I know this? Because other people gossip to me and tell me. Will I be as forthcoming to work with those people again? Probably not. Any opportunities I have that I would once have gladly shared with these people, I will longer share.

One time I was a partner in a venture capital firm. I thought one of the companies was being poorly run and I wanted to replace the CEO. Instead of just discussing this rationally with my partners, I went "above and beyond" and trashed the CEO in various ways that were inappropriate. As these things usually happen, I was scheduled to have dinner with the CEO that night. He came over my house and we were all ready to go out to eat, wives and all. First thing he did, he repeated verbatim what I had said in private to my partners. Ugh. Awkward dinner. Awkward thousands of moments I had to deal with him afterwards.

Another story: a good friend of mine was taking her coffee break at work. She said some gossip about a co-worker. She turns around and there's the co-worker, looking at her. My friend was horrified. She apologized profusely. She sent an email. She was super nice to the person she was gossiping about. Months went by. I saw her at one point and she said, "I don't understand! I apologized. I did this, this, and this for her. Why is she still mad at me?" Answer: because she is. You can't change what people think of you. But you can change your need, our species' natural addiction, to harmful gossip.

I've seen people gossip even worse: about their bosses or about their clients. Of course the bosses or clients find out. Then the employees are either fired or moved into positions where their advancement is unlikely. Or other situations: if I was an employee and someone was gossiping about our boss, I'd slowly back off and get away and *stay away* from that employee. I don't want to have the "guilt-by-association" thing on me.

What happens when you stop gossiping? You have more time (gossiping consumes a lot of time). You have more friends. You have no risk of insulting the people who you otherwise would have insulted. And you gradually move ahead in the ranks of everyone who succumbed the shortcomings of gossip.

What about gossiping about people in other companies? This is almost as bad. The average amount of time people spend at a job is now around 3 years. Many industries are somewhat incestuous. One day you work at Company A, the next day you work at a competitor, Company B. And so on. The person you gossip about today could be your officemate tomorrow. And then your growth in that industry will be hindered. Don't do it.

· · · · · ✳ · · · · ·

A RICH EMPLOYEE ASKS AT THE END OF EVERY DAY: WHO DID I HELP TODAY?

Without reading it, many people accused me of writing: *"Choose Yourself!"* because in their opinion it glorified selfishness. I would just say, "read it".

The exact opposite is true. You cannot help others choose themselves until you have chosen yourself to be healthy, to be free from the gatekeepers, to have a life of freedom.

Right now, we are still coming out of a 200-year period of "Corporatism". Big corporations wanted employees to all be taught the same way, paid the same way, live close by, be dependent on the corporation.

This was never the intent of capitalism. A free economy is not about giving all of your value in exchange for a paycheck. That's just another form of bribery.

The reason I know this is simple: the economy is growing and paychecks versus inflation are going down. This is because the era of Corporatism is over but the era of "Idea-ism" is just beginning. Everything but ideas can be outsourced. Software development, design, accounting, translation, research. Almost everything you can go to school for, you can now outsource.

Except you can't outsource your ability to build and deepen relationships. You can't outsource "you". I ask my kids every day, "Who did you help today?" At first they were like, "What?" But then when they thought about it they would start to come up with answers. Then it became easier when they knew throughout the day that it was going to end with me asking them that question.

Think about Google for a second. Why do you always return to Google to do your searches, particularly when there was more competition when they first started out? It's because they helped you more. If you typed in "motorcycles" to Google as opposed to Excite, you would get better results, and usually faster. Google measured their success by how quickly you left their site. Probably the only website to do that. But when you had to go back and do a search, you didn't go back to the motorcycle website (particularly if you were searching for "boats"), and you didn't go back to Excite (because a lot of the sites they linked to were of no help at all), you went back to Google. Now Google has $64 billion in cash in the bank.

One befit of getting to work early each day and getting most of your work done is that you can then spend part of the day figuring out how to help your co-workers. You create an exquisite web of work connections where you are the spider in the middle. I don't mean this in an insidious way but in a beautiful way.

I was visiting Michael Singer, author of the mega-bestseller, "*The Untethered Soul*", a beautiful book that was prominently featured on Oprah. He has given only two in-person interviews about his books. One to Oprah and one to Claudia and me. So I was very grateful.

What many people did not know about Michael until his latest book: "*The Surrender Experiment*" came out was that he also built up a multi-billion dollar company from scratch that ultimately merged with WebMD. You would not know that by visiting him. He lives in the same house he's lived in for decades and he devotes his life to helping others achieve some measure of peace in their lives through his writings and his in-person teachings on the land and buildings he's bought up where his old company used to be.

He was giving Claudia and me the tour of his thousand acres of land and the various buildings he's built along the way. At one point I saw an enormous spider, probably the biggest spider I had ever seen, that had spun a web all the way across the front of his house. We had to walk around the web to get in. But first, Michael said to me, "Come over here and touch the web." I touched the outer fringes of the web. It moved under my touch.

Michael said: "this web has stronger tensile strength than steel". Tensile strength means the ability to break it. You might not think it because spider webs are so thin they are easy to break if you slash right through them. But a string of spider silk has a diameter of 3-6 micrometers (1 millionth of a meter) and is 1/6 the density of steel. When you help people, you weave the web, you build a connection between you and the other person that is incredibly strong.

Robert Cialdini demonstrates this further in his masterpiece on marketing called: "*Influence*". He tells the story of when the Hari Krishna group was first trying to raise money in airports they were failing miserably. They made one small change to what they were doing. They handed you a flower first. They raised hundreds of millions after that. Nobody really wanted the flower. In fact, most people would throw them in the nearest garbage can. Guess what? Hari Krishna members would fetch the flowers out of the garbage cans and re-hand them out. Cialdini calls this phenomenon the "Law of Reciprocity". The cognitive bias we have to help people who give something to us. It becomes much harder to say "no" to someone if they have just done something for you. This sounds manipulative and if you approach it in a totally manipulative way it still might work (think: Hari Krishna) but even better is if you sincerely listen to other people's problems, help them, become a resource, and become the center of the web. Next time I see a Hari Krishna with a flower I might avoid them.

I use Google for every search and that's how Google has become one of the most valuable companies on the planet with it's two founders being among the richest people who ever lived.

Ultimately what happens is that if you have a mindset of "Who can I help today?" you will become indispensable to the company you are working for. If you help not just the colleagues in your group, but your boss, the managers of other divisions, the customers, the shareholders - whatever group you can that is connected to your company, then you start to tie your success further to the company. If you remain an employee and don't take the entrepreneurial route you have to work for a company that is willing to tie your success to their success. Many companies do not currently do that. Why? Because many companies (and employees) are under the mistaken belief that in exchange for accepting a secure salary (every two weeks, on the dot, never goes away, goes up with inflation every year), you owe the company your loyalty and value.

As I mentioned in the beginning of this book, this is simply not true. Many things can go wrong along the way. You *want* your salary to be volatile and have the opportunity for great riches. And, in reality, that is actually the safer route to go.

Corporate culture in America is moving towards an environment where the salary is safe...until it isn't, until it can be outsourced. But what can't be outsourced, almost by definition, are the employees who have proven themselves indispensable because their ability to help more and more constituencies of the company. In other words, you.

Note that the more stable a salary is, the less useful it is. If you always know you are going to get a salary, you may be lulled into thinking you can work less. In other words, your salary is not giving you any feedback on whether your performance is good or bad. For the employee who ties his financial status to the financial status of the company, then your ultimate wealth is much more volatile. When you lose money it's because you might have done something incorrectly. This is feedback you can use to make more money. And when you make more money, this is feedback that you are doing good things.

The universe is chaotic and volatile. Anything that tries to cover that up with makeup and a mask is only fooling themselves. The costume party is over at the end of the night.

····· ✳ ·····

A RICH EMPLOYEE GIVES CREDIT TO HIS BOSSES AND EMPLOYERS

I had a mentor in college who taught me several valuable lessons that have helped me throughout my life since then. By the way, nothing related to education at all. His courses were useless. I never once made use of anything I actually learned from his classes. I learned more from how he conducted his career, things that I've used to create my own career.

1) HE CHOSE HIMSELF

He was a professor of computer science but he didn't start off that way. He got a PhD in theoretical physics. When he was working on his thesis, Stephen Hawking said to him: "if you solve this problem, it will change the game in physics." Then, when he did in fact solve the problem, Stephen Hawking said: "Hmmm, I guess it wasn't as important as I initially thought." Disappointed, he moved from Utah to New York, and became obsessed with computer science. He would sit in on classes, read all the books, program, etc. Then he wanted to be a professor but Cornell said "no". So Prakash found a classroom that was empty in the early evenings and put up signs that said: "Lectures on Programming Languages" and gave the time and day. At first a few people would show up. Then more. Then more. He was an excellent teacher.

Finally, so many students were attending his lectures that Cornell had to make him a professor. Later he got tenure. Then later he moved to a chaired professorship at another school where he still teaches. He didn't let the gate-keepers tell him "no" and he eventually worked his dream job.

2) He Judged His Success by the Success of his Students

He was not a well-known professor. He never published any world-shaking papers. But all of his students have gone on to be very successful professors. He told me specifically: "my success will be so if I have successful students". He always gave them full credit for everything and helped them in every aspect of their careers.

3) He Taught Me How to Speak

One of the most worthless things I've ever done was write an academic research paper. One time Prakash and I were working together on the project, we co-wrote the paper and got accepted to present it at the most prestigious conference in our industry. So we both flew out to Kaiserslautern, Germany and, true to form, he was going to let me do the presentation.

The night before the presentation to the whole conference there was a conference dinner - a chance for networking, new friendships, to learn about the projects of others, and good food. Instead, Prakash said: "those are boring. Let's go to the conference hall." We went to the empty conference hall and he said, "Let me see your slides." He saw them and said, "this is awful" and we rewrote all of them. Then he said, "Ok, let me see you give the talk."

For each slide, we went over and over the talk while I was up on the stage and he was the only person in the audience. He would have me re-do jokes, re-do when I moved around, re-do when I looked at the audience as opposed to when I focused on the slides. We were there for hours. Before this presentation I was never able to give a good talk. During the presentation, I had people laughing. People even came up to me afterwards and said, "I never understood that topic before. Can you give the same talk at our university." Which is saying something when I tell you the topic of the talk and the paper, "Automatically proving the adjoint-functor theorem in category theory". VERY useless.

4) HE ALWAYS GAVE CREDIT TO HIS STUDENTS

We walked through the streets of Kaiserslautern on our way to our respective hotels after he had me practice the talk. Before we split off he gave a final piece of advice: "don't go to any porn shops in Germany. They will rip you off." That's the last I ever saw him. A year later I was thrown out of graduate school. But the thing that sticks the most, always give credit to others. In Prakash's case he always gave credit to his students.

It works in both directions. Your manager is also an employee at a job. He often has to manage upwards as well as downwards. Downwards to you but upwards to his manager, his manager's manager, the shareholders, the customers, and so on. All the usual suspects. He or she needs your help. When you do something good, they will want to take credit for it. They want to look good. The Rich Employee doesn't care about taking credit. The Rich Employee creates so much value he/she has credit to spare and can easily just outright give it to others. Not even share it. Give it. This makes everyone up the chain look good. And again, it further ties your success to the success of everyone above you.

In one job I had, I was always giving my manager credit for everything. Finally he got a huge promotion. Instead of everyone congratulating his well-deserved title and salary increase, everyone stopped by my cubicle and congratulated me because they knew I had greatly helped my manager to shine and define an entire new industry for the company. When I was later starting my own company on the side, did my manager try to stop me? Of course not! Again, *reciprocity*. I was indispensable to his career and I built up a significant business from my little cubicle until, with a dozen employees and on track for seven figures in revenues I finally quit and became CEO of my first company.

· · · · · ✳ · · · · ·

The Rich Employee Focuses on Mission and Long-Range Profits

A company doesn't just come up with a product, determine price, and then start selling.

A company identifies an urgent problem, develops a unique solution, and only then makes it affordable, easy to use, and starts to market that product to customers.

And often it fails. Or the world changes. Or the experiment of releasing one product didn't work but another product did.

Amazon is a great example. Jeff Bezos didn't want to just sell books. He wanted to sell everything. Nobody would believe him so he started off with a simple story: "I want to sell books online". And it worked. He quickly became the biggest online bookseller. In fact, some people thought this was so unimportant they outsourced their online book sales to Amazon. Remember Borders?

Now Amazon sells food, clothes, music, and even makes original TV shows.

Do they make money? No! Of course not. Because they are constantly building. Will they make money eventually? Yes, they will.

But guess what happened along the way. In fact, it happened today – the day I am writing this chapter. Amazon's market capitalization passed that of the largest retailer in the world: Walmart. The future is here.

And it was defined by one man's mission without thought of how quickly he could cash out and squeeze profits out of the customer.

In my own company where I make some of my content, premium content, I have one value that is above all other values:

····· ✳ ·····

MESSAGE FIRST

I know that if I can deliver a message that actually helps people in this chaotic world, than money will be a byproduct of that in the long run.

For every decision we have to make at the company, for every product, for every sales letter, we always ask the question – is this putting the message first.

How do you do this if you are an employee? How do you have a set of "employee values"?

First make sure your own personal values match the values of the company you work for.

Second, I would start to define what is most important to you in any work situation. Do you value honesty over salary. Do you value helping others versus getting out of work early? Do you value having time to research and learn as opposed to putting in 12 hours a day so you can rise up the corporate ladder.

It's ok if you don't. Maybe you want to get out early to spend more time with your kids. That's great. But then you have to find a job or a source of income that aligns with that.

Write down what your long-term values are. When they closely match your work situation, this is how you align your financial success with the success of the company.

Once you do this you are primed to make an enormous amount of money as your company succeeds.

······ ❋ ······

The Rich Employee Is Constantly Learning about the Competitors, the Industry, the History

Either as a job, a startup, a side gig, an advisor, or an investor, I've been involved in about 15 different industries. Maybe more. I say this because in some of those industries I failed and some I succeeded. One time I failed HORRIBLY (millions gained, then millions lost) because I did not understand the business at all. So this is not about what you need to learn but an example of what I DIDN'T learn that caused me to fail and what could have been a lifetime opportunity (millions gained! before millions lost (sad face)).

First off, more specifics: I was an advisor to the company. My success was tied to the success of the company. I was advising on how they should change their brand and message themselves and also I advised on how they should communicate to employees and use social media. All good. They took my advice and did very well with it (hence the initial millions). But since I had the ear of the CEO and the board based on my initial success with them, I could've maybe been a lot more useful, particularly when they were flirting with disaster and ultimately died with disaster.

A. I didn't really know who their competitors were. I had a vague idea of who the major players were but not a subtle understand of the demographics of the customers and services and how it compared with the major players.

B. I never fully understood all the services they supplied to their customers. This was critical. How could I give advice without fully knowing the product?

C. I never went over their accounting with a microscope. Accounting is not just about how cash comes in and goes out. You have to understand the subtleties of how a company depreciates the assets they own, what expectations lenders have on the company, what could cause a death spiral if certain conditions happen (loss of a customer or a vendor or a lender), etc.

D. I didn't understand the exact nature of their vendor relationships. I never even looked at a single written deal with their vendors and how they worked.

E. I didn't know the history of the space and how it constantly changed based on government regulations. I should have understood completely the history of M&A transactions in the space, the cyclical nature of the industry, how the industry survived in recessions, etc.

F. I didn't fully understand the personal histories of their leaders and their largest shareholders. Since I had so much access to their management I could've sat down with each one and conducted a full interview as to their backgrounds, where they worked, and maybe even struck gold on what their personal issues and dreams were at that point.

G. I had a vague grasp of industry trends in the future, which is how I was able to provide the advice they asked for. But I think I could've done a much better job at understanding the deeper meaning of these trends if I had learned all of the above.

The company's failure was not my fault. But, perhaps I could've been of better service (or had more knowledge about cashing out) if I had understood all of these things. I mention this not to underline how miserable at this job I was, but rather as an example of how there is always room to learn. And if you have money and meaning and value on the line, these things that seem ancillary to the service you are providing with your job become more important than ever.

For all the items I listed above: If I had known the answer, it would have made millions of dollars difference in my bank account. As it stands, I made nothing from that business I was so heavily involved in.

On *every* other occasion where I have made millions of dollars, I knew the questions to all of the above. In fact, I was obsessed with these details. Perhaps I just didn't care enough in this one particular industry. And it's not even about money but about competence, relationships, and freedom.

When I had a job at HBO I knew all of the answers to the above, even when my managers and my colleagues did not. What did that mean for me? It meant I was able to propose products (a website with original programming, for instance) that established my competence, built up strong relationships with other constituencies within the company, and ultimately have the freedom to start my own company on the side while continuing to make more and more money at HBO. I loved HBO's product. I read or watched or listened to all Time Warner products. I understood inside and out the cable business, even the satellite business. I understood the accounting of how subscriber acquisition cash flow sometimes didn't match (in GAAP accounting) subscriber acquisition revenues. I studied the personal histories of every manager. I studied the history of the company. I watched closely how the industry was slowly moving in the direction of HBO (the first "movie channel" to do original programming) until now even Netflix, Amazon, and other cable companies have followed their model. It's no wonder that ex-HBO employees are behind the scenes at almost every other company that does original programming, including tech giants like Netflix and Amazon.

When I started an internet business, I went through the same process. When I started a hedge fund I also went through the same process.

You have to do be the greatest expert in the field to dominate an industry. In "Choose Yourself" I describe the story of Bryan Johnson, who studied all the flaws (and then publicly documented those flaws) when he started Braintree, a credit card payments processor. Braintree has since sold for well over a billion dollars and it was precisely because he knew all the nuances that he was able to wipe out all the competition.

Whether you are an employee or an entrepreneur or somewhere in the middle, this is one of the most critical factors that separate out the people who will make millions or find meaning in their positions, as opposed to the Poor Employee mindset where you go in for the quick and easy paycheck and hope to get out alive before it is taken from you. Unfortunately, paycheck and freedom have been taken from me far too many times when I ignored this simple principle that I can no longer afford, literally, to forget about it. A shorter way to have said this would be to simply write, "Information is Power" but often people don't know what information to get. I didn't, and it cost me.

· · · · · ✳ · · · · ·

The Rich Employee Has New Ideas Every Day, Knows How to Execute Them

"Ideas are a dime a dozen. Execution is everything". I actually sort of believe this despite my emphasis on the importance of developing the "idea muscle", but with some caveats. As I've said before, the idea muscle needs to be constantly exercised. If it doesn't, it atrophies until you are no longer successful at coming up with good ideas.

I'm in a fortunate position. Because I've written so much about it (two books, plus Claudia's book on this topic) people send me their ideas all the time to take a look at. Also, people send me testimonials. I'm able to tell immediately who has been exercising this idea muscle and who hasn't. Who really pushes themselves when coming up with ideas, and who gives up quickly and goes for the easy way out. I can say, "my life has changed every six months" since starting this practice and you can decide whether or not to believe me. But now on Quora, Facebook, and in Choose Yourself Meetups around the world you can easily find discussions of people who have been doing this exercise of writing down ten ideas a day and what the results have been.

My first caveat: Ideas are not quite a dime a dozen. They are a dime for three or four. If I wanted to come up with, say, "ten ideas for Facebook" maybe I can come up with a quick three. But to come up with ten ideas that I think are good (whether or not they are good is another thing, but I have to think they are good at the very least), it starts get hard right around four or five and almost impossible around seven. This is where the burn starts. Where you are really exercising that idea muscle.

People ask me, "How do I know if I have a good idea?" You don't really. But the more you do this, the better ideas you will have *all the time*.

As to execution, how does one execute? Execution ideas are a subset of coming up with ideas. I might have an idea for a new app that keeps track of what stores I'm passing on my daily walks and offers to find me deals on the Internet that are cheaper than what is being sold in the stores. This may or may not be a good idea. I'm just thinking out loud. And of course, thinking gets me know where. The smartest people alive, who never executed, are never heard of again. Only action makes a hero. Superman never sat around in his living room and said, "Hmmm, should I help Lois?" No. He had to change clothes, jump out of his window and grab her repeatedly while she fell through the air. Almost every day. Execution saved Lois's life.

Here's how you do it: once you have an idea you feel like executing on, write down "10 easy execution steps for this idea". Maybe spec out each page. Maybe outsource a developer on freelancer.com to spec out each page, or draw each page, or create one page with functionality, and so on. Then, if the steps are easy enough, pick one, and just spend ten minutes doing it (let's say I want someone to format this book (so I can execute, i.e. publish it). I can simply put on freelancer or fiver, "need to publish on Amazon. Will hire someone to format my book for the kindle". That's an execution step. A string of those and then the book is published.

· · · · · ✳ · · · · ·

THE RICH EMPLOYEE — BUILDS DEEPER BONDS WITH EMPLOYEES ALL ACROSS THE COMPANY

The Rich Employee knows that power is not with the managers but with the secretaries. The secretaries are the gatekeepers within the company. Whether it's information or access you want to the various managers in each division, it's important to get buy-in from the people who work for them. A counter-example is: you can't just walk into the CEO's office. First you have to cultivate all the relationships underneath the CEO. Then when you are ready, when you have the right ideas, the doors to the CEO's office will be open to you.

· · · · · ✳ · · · · ·

THE RICH EMPLOYEE WORKS FOR A COMPANY THAT ALLOWS FOR ALL OF THE ABOVE

Some companies are stuck in their ways. They want factory workers that they can pay every two weeks and have the right to fire them at a moment's notice once technology inevitably devours their jobs.

For companies to succeed, they need to cultivate the Rich Employee mindset. Else, eventually, their cultures will change, their employees will be weak and resistant to change, their managers (promoted from their ranks) will prove to be less adaptable and less understanding of the changes around them, and the companies will fall apart. A culture of success ties the success of everyone in the company to the results of the company.

There is plenty of anecdotal evidence of this: Google, Microsoft, Apple, Procter & Gamble, all created millionaires out of their employees by paying employees in stock or options in the company. These companies went on to become among the most successful companies ever.

But let's just look at the facts that we all know. The gap between rich and poor is getting bigger all across the world. I am not making a judgment on this, nor is this something that can be regulated away by new laws. What is the difference between the wealthy that are "going up" and the poor that seem to be "going down". We know that income versus inflation is going down. You get income when you work at a job with a steady paycheck. And yet, the stock markets around the world are at or near all-time highs. And even if they have a collapse like in 2009, it only took six years before they were at all time highs again. So that leads to one conclusion: the people who OWN are getting wealthier. The people who sacrificed ownership for the myth of stability are getting poorer.

In the book, *"The Citizens Share"*, which came out in 2014, authors Joseph Blasi, Richard Freeman, and Douglas Kruse site example after example from the 1800s until now where employee ownership was directly correlated with employee happiness, higher innovation at the company, and greater profits and stock market prices. That's just ownership. But there are many ways to tie your success to the success of your company: you can be paid in money, of course, which is good. But also in freedom, in well-being, in better opportunities for your future, and so on. If the company consistently clamps on this, then the Rich Employee knows to move on.

····· ❋ ·····

THE RICH EMPLOYEE HELPS HIS/HER
EMPLOYEES SUCCEED

The Rich Employee must become a *leader*. This is a theme throughout this book. Again, it doesn't matter how much you know about all the latest tricks, and Internet marketing techniques, and latest apps that can help productivity. All of these principles work throughout all time and they will continue to work. Of course, part of that is knowing the latest and greatest that can help you. But 90% of it, is understanding these deeper principles.

As you grow in wealth, responsibilities, competence, relationships, and whether or not you grow in your job or start to have more and more opportunities for side income, you need to become a leader. I am the best bad leader in the world. Not only do I know everything about how to fail as a leader but I also have spent large amounts of time with bad leaders. All the time I read articles titled something like: *"Top 10 Qualities of GREAT Leaders"*.

Why do people write these articles? Were they great leaders? I have no idea. In most cases it doesn't seem so. It seems like they are leaders of writing a lot of articles about leaders. Study is one thing, writing is the next thing, but doing and then repeating is how you learn.

So why do they write these articles? Many reasons and I applaud them for all of those reasons. They write them to get name recognition. They write them to get consulting gigs. To be a life coach maybe to other leaders or CEOs. They write them to get speaking gigs. And that technique works. I know this. If you write enough articles about leadership, someone will pay you to teach them how to be a leader. Try it and you'll see. But I have to stick with what I know. I know a thing or two about good leadership. Good leadership is very rare. I can count a list of good leaders on my two hands. Larry Page is a good leader. Winston Churchill is a good leader.

I have known and worked with for many bad leaders. Plus I have been a bad leader many times in my life. I don't know if I'd be a good leader now. But I do know the mistakes I made that caused me to crash and burn in leadership. Sometimes, to be a little bit better, you just have to avoid the little bit worse.

So let's get started.

····· ❋ ·····

THE QUALITIES OF A BAD LEADER

A) NOT UNDERSTANDING THE 30/150 RULE

A leader has to follow the 30/150 rule or they will be a bad leader. This rule has worked for 200,000 years. If a rule works for 2 years then ignore it. If a rule has worked for 200,000 years then pay attention to it. For 200,000 years humans were tribes. Every tribe had a leader but when the tribe got too big for one leader (more than 30 people), it would split in two. Then, around 70,000 years ago we evolved to handle tribes up to 150 people. Then maybe 10,000 years ago we figured out how to be above 150 people. But this is so new, an evolutionary blip, that we screw it up all the time.

But for each of these three categories (< 30 people, < 150 people, > 150 people) give bad leaders an opportunity to prove how bad they are. I'll tell you how right now. A bad leader will not change his behavior no matter how many people he or she leads.

B) UNDER 30 PEOPLE. AVOIDING ONE ON ONE GIVING

If you are a leader of less than 30 people, you have to know intimately the problems of all 30 people (or less) in your organization. You have to know their skills. What they are good at. What they are bad at. What they want to be good at. What their dreams are.

Each person should be assigned ONE thing. That's their responsibility. Bad leaders give people many things and then those people do mediocre jobs at all of them instead of being responsible for their one special egg they have to carry from one side of the room to the other on a spoon. When I was running a company with less than 30 people I would take random employees with me to meetings. So this way they would see the effect the company had on our clients or other people would deal with. My goal: I knew I had limitations as a leader. So I wanted my employees to be leaders. Bad leaders get jealous of the people underneath them and never hire people smarter than them. This is the #1 most common thing a bad leader does.

Understand each of the 30 people at an intimate level. Know who their parents are. Know what they do for fun. Help them maximize their skills. Make them succeed and shine past you. This maybe is the one time I was a decent leader. I don't know. But, to this day, I still know and am friends with each one of those 30. Give to them more than they give to you and they will still be giving to you 20 years later. This I know for a fact.

C) ABOVE 30 PEOPLE, BUT BELOW 150.
HOW TO SCREW IT UP.

When your organization is between 30 and 150, it's impossible for you to know everyone. So make sure everyone is talking about everyone else. I want to be able to ask A what B is like to work with and I want a real good answer. The people reporting directly to you should be giving more than they are getting to the people working for them. That's how you get to know people.

That is how the leader, indirectly, gets to know the entire 150 when he or she is putting together teams and assignments and trying to inspire people for a common goal.

D) FAILING THE "VISION THING"

Above 150 people you need to do many things. But here's the #1 thing leaders fail at. No vision.

What's a vision? I suppose a 1000 boring books can be written about this. Let's hold off for a second on defining it. But above 150, it's impossible to know everyone in your organization or even know second-hand about everyone in your organization. So the most important thing you can do, in fact the ONLY thing you can do, is lead by example. For instance, what if 50,000 people are in your organization, or, in the case of the President of the United States, 300 million people.

You can't unify the people by talking to each one and understanding their problems. You can't define roles and fulfill dreams for people by talking to others who know everyone. You have to unify them with a story. A story everyone believes in and is inspired by and is willing to follow. So if you and I believe in the Yankees, we're more likely to trust each other than if I like the Yankees and you like the Mets.

All stories: religions, nationalism, politics, issues, etc. are more or less designed to figure out how to unify the greatest number of people with the strongest ties possible. Because we are not so good at it, often this degrades into wars, or poor leadership, or things just disappear into the furnace of time.

When Tim Cook became CEO of Apple, everyone was afraid the story would change. The stock dropped. What was the story? It wasn't that Steve Jobs "gets the most profits". A story is rarely about money (although money itself is probably the strongest story on the planet). It's that Steve Jobs had the greatest combination of "technology + design". Could Tim Cook keep that story going? Tim Cook's leadership will be entirely judged on whether he keeps that story going or if he can successfully change the story. Actually, he has to do both. Because if he tries to turn himself into Steve Jobs then he will be judged on the story of: "is Tim Cook just a bad version of Steve Jobs." So it's a delicate balance. One that has to be dealt with every day in order for him to attract the best employees, keep his customers happy, keep his investors happy, and probably to keep himself happy. This is leadership.

E) Having a Bad Vision

Okay, let's get closer to defining a bad vision. Good visions are difficult to come up with. It's pretty rare. But since I know so many bad leaders I can tell you first an example of bad visions. I've been in the management of at least two companies worth over a billion dollars. In both cases, leadership was horrible. How did they get to a billion dollars with such bad leadership? Easy. Anyone can do that part. I will tell you how. They went public on the stock market and then used their shares to buy other companies. Every city has a smaller version that can be acquired by the bigger version. So buy a lot of smaller versions of you and you add up the numbers and suddenly you have a billion in revenues.

But your only vision was: "we just bought a lot of companies that do the same thing and now we have a billion dollars in revenues!" Ach! Your vision might even be worse than that. It might be "We just bought a lot of companies, fired all of the HR people and accounting people (because we had them in the main office) and now we have a billion in revenues and even greater profits and margins!" Every company that has ever done that has failed. Some companies did that and came close to failing. For example, Google never had a chance of failing. But they were buying a company a week when Eric Schmidt was the CEO. They weren't quite bringing these companies in under the fold correctly and Google was starting to flounder. Divisions were being shut down. Morale was at a low because the vision of Google was starting to flounder. Larry Page took over and changed the story. He said, "Google is the best in the world at these four things" and he closed down everything that wasn't part of one of those four silos. Everyone left in one of those silos can now say, "We are the best in the world at this" and that contributes to the larger vision of Google of having the entirety of world information at your fingertips wherever you are: The first company in world history to do this.

Man, I wish I worked at Google, to be honest. It almost happened once when I tried to sell a company to them. I loved their vision so much I wanted to bathe every inch of my body in it. I wanted to be religious about it. And that's what all great religious leaders do. They tell a story. Some elements of a good story:

We fight an evil force (think the Apple 1984 commercial against IBM. Think Buddha rejecting the caste system. Think Washington rejecting a third term because he didn't want the Presidency to turn into a monarchy). We have something mysterious that nobody else has (a deity, better design philosophy, better technology, etc.). We think people will be happier if they work with us, subscribe to us, and join us. Apple often has inferior products to other comparable products. But people are actually happier with an Apple product because the story is so strong.

Our leaders have "seen the light" or "come out from the cold". Steve Jobs had to leave his company for a decade in order to come back a hero. Buddha had to leave his home for seven years to achieve enlightenment. Mandela was in jail for decades.

Together we are better than apart. The bigger we are, the better we can help people who join us. So, if a company is buying lots of smaller companies, they need a vision that explains why bigger is better. For instance, we're able to help people faster because we understand the needs in every city in the world.

Social proof: A vision should have other stories within it. People your vision has helped, people whose lives became better. People who can stand up and say, "this changed my life". Bad corporate leaders will do this: buy all the companies, fire all the waste, report good numbers to the stock market, and then sell their stock, the stock goes down, the company falls apart. I've seen that happen a lot.

F) Bad Leaders Don't Want You to Call Your Mother

Every day, the people following a good leader should be able to call their parents and say, "I'm happy. You won't believe what I did/learned/met today."

G) Bad Leaders Talk Badly About Their Clients or Employees or Constituents

I was giving a talk at one company. It turns out they mostly hated their clients. I was surprised. How can you hate your clients? They are the ones who pay you money. They are the reason you come into work. If you hate what your clients' story is, how you can help them achieve their dreams.

Something will always block you from performing the best service for them. Leadership is not about achieving your dream. It's about helping everyone else achieve their dreams.

This is not the employees' fault. Everything comes from the leaders. If the leader doesn't love the clients/constituents then the people below the leader and the people below them won't. Trickle-down leadership is the only leadership.

II) Bad Leaders Don't Want You to Pass Them

I've had four mentors in my life. Some people tried to be a mentor also but they didn't quite have that *mentor-ish* effect on me. What do I mean by that? It means I wanted to be like them. I wanted my life path to mirror theirs. I wanted to mimic their behavior and learn their knowledge so I could be as successful as them. I've had many more teachers than four. But maybe only four mentors.

And here's what happened to each one of them: they all wanted me to fail at some point. That's a bad mentor. I learned what I could from them. I did everything they asked. I helped each one of them with their continual successes. But at some point, when I wanted to go on my own and learn more and start my own business or direction, they all were angry and they all tried to stop me and none of them talk to me anymore. In two cases, they actively tried to damage me even though I had never done anything but help them. It even gets worse but I don't want to put anyone down. I was aware of the dangers and went into it willingly.

A good leader helps the people around them succeed past them. A great example is Stanford professor, Rajeev Montwani. What!? Who is he? Well, he was Sergey Brin's advisor. And instead of trying to keep Brin in a cage, he opened the cage and Brin flew out and started Google with fellow grad student Larry Page. Now Montwani is a billionaire as a result.

Leadership doesn't ask the question "How good can I get? How far can I get?"

Leadership asks the question "How far can the people around me get?"

People always say negative things about Steve Jobs, because of unfair media portrayals of him. But if Steve Jobs were such a bad person he wouldn't have been as great a leader. People like Tim Cook, Jony Ive, John Lasseter (from Pixar) and many others (even Bob Iger, the CEO of Disney), Tony Fadell (developer of the iPod, who just sold Nest for $3.2 billion to Google) owe huge amounts of their success, their creativity, the distribution of their creativity, and their freedom and well-being, to the fact that at one point or other they were mentored by Steve Jobs or benefited from leadership decisions made by Steve Jobs.

All of these people were very self-motivated, which is how they found themselves with someone like Steve Jobs as a mentor. Combine that self-motivation with the leadership skills of Steve Jobs and you end up with great success.

The same thing happened at Google with the leadership skills of Larry Page.

The CEOs or COOs of Twitter, Facebook, AOL, and Yahoo all were at one point mentees of Larry Page and are now successful leaders and mentors themselves.

I) Bad Leaders Don't Know Their Numbers

I'm raising my hand. When I ran companies it took me a long time to realize what numbers I needed to know. For instance, when you run a company you need to know not only your revenues and earnings but also your revenues and earnings per employee, per customer, per square foot, etc. This applies whether you are the leader of a company, of a meetup group, of a country, of anything.

What are the metrics you need to know to determine success? If you are the teacher of a class, come up with a list of things you hope your students achieve by the end of the class. Not all of them will achieve it. That's okay. List each student. Next to each student's name, list all of the things you want them to achieve. At the beginning of the class, list each item for each student on a scale of 1-10. Add up all the numbers for all students so you have one final number. This is the number you are starting with. By the time the class is over, that number should be higher. It might mean just one student succeeded greatly. That's okay. Then you were a good leader.

If you are having a hard time coming up with the right metrics, just use these:

- COMPETENCE,
- RELATIONSHIPS, AND
- AUTONOMY.

Help each person get better at those three things. By the way, it's important to have metrics. I visited a company recently that I felt had a bad vision for their customers. Bad metrics used to define the success of their customers. But even a bad vision is better than no vision.

J) BAD LEADERS DON'T GET RID OF BAD PEOPLE

I was involved with a company once that had a weak leader. He owed his leadership to the largest shareholder of the company. The problem is: the largest shareholder of the company was hideously corrupt. The good leader should have disassociated himself from the large shareholder, built a vision around his own leadership. Instead, he became mired in the financial difficulties of the largest shareholder, was unable to unify the divisions underneath him and provide effective mentorship to the people who directly worked for him. The company fell apart a year after he took over as CEO.

Bad leadership, no matter what the situation, can cause almost instantaneous collapse. The 2008 failures of Bear Stearns and Lehman Brothers are great examples. When Bear Stearns stock price was falling from $80 to $2 within the space of a week, the CEO was off playing in a bridge tournament. Bridge is a card game. While he was playing cards, thousands of employees lost their jobs. And the downfall of Bear Stearns triggered the dominos that ultimately led to the multi trillion-dollar bailouts of all banks and insurance firms that happened over the next ten months after the fall of Bear Stearns. Ultimately, the person who had installed him to be leader of Bear Stearns should've removed him or recognized his own character defects. Here's the problem with that and I'll mention it in the next point...

K) A Bad Leader Often Has Enormous Charisma

How can someone who is a bad leader reach a leadership position? Easy. They have enormous charisma. They are insanely smart and know how to charm the leaders who came before them. A great example might be the set of a movie production. The director is the leader. But he has a big problem. Actors are hired because of their enormous (ENORMOUS) charisma. The world loves them. So when they want something, it's hard to say "no" to them. A good director has to fight the urge to succumb to the charisma of the people he is leading and stay focused on the vision.

For instance, in the case of Bear Stearns, the intoxication happened the instant the original leader, Alan Greenberg, met the new guy. Jim Cayne, the new guy, was a professional bridge player. In fact, that's all he was. To play bridge well (to play any professional-level game well) you need years of study, you need to be able to read people very well, you need to know numbers very well and to calculate many situations in your head quickly. All of these things are attributes of good leaders and so those tools can often fool other good leaders into thinking you are a good leader. But unfortunately for everyone, Jim Cayne was JUST a good bridge player and was not good at anything else. Many good leaders who are successful game players include Bill Gates (bridge), Warren Buffett (bridge), Peter Thiel (chess), and numerous others. Alan Greenberg was an aspiring bridge player. He met Jim Cayne, who was a great bridge player. He asked Jim, "How good are you?" and Jim said, "if you played me for 100 years you will never be able to beat me." That began the road to success for Cayne and then the entire collapse of the American economy.

L) BAD LEADERS SMOKE CRACK

I don't mean literally. Although if they did smoke crack they'd probably never get to a real leadership position. There's a cognitive bias that causes people to not see their own failings. They've spent so much time, effort, and money creating their particular vision that they have "investment bias" that prevents their brains from saying, "maybe I've made a mistake".

A bad leader will not admit his faults or even think about them. It's too painful to think about those faults because of this cognitive bias. The brain will revolt or the leader will get depressed or start to doubt his leadership skills.

One time I was starting a company at the same as a friend of mine. I knew instantly his company was bad but, perhaps I was not a good enough friend,

I didn't tell him his idea was bad. Instead I would question him: who are the users? Who are the customers? How will you make money? I wanted him to see for himself through my questions that his idea was bad. But because I was asking these questions it sort of "woke me up". Every day I would ask myself the same questions about my own company. Every day I would call my partners and ask them, "am I smoking crack?" and I would go over the questions with them. This process forced me to outline new features every day that could help me provide better services to my customers. I sold my business eight months to the day after I started it for $10,000,000. My friend's business: nine years later he's still pushing it. It has zero revenues.

You have to step outside yourself and do due diligence on your own organization as if you were an outsider. Come up in advance, all of the metrics of success. Decide if those are the correct metrics. You have to assume you are smoking crack because often you will be. You can't help it. We're all human. So get help from others in your organization. Get help from customers. Get help from people outside the organization. They won't always be right either. And sometimes they will lie to you just to avoid being hurtful to your dreams (just like I was with my friend). The only person who can ultimately prevent you from smoking crack is you. This separates the good leaders from the bad leaders in many cases.

M) Bad Leaders Were Bad Employees

Leadership starts long before you reach the top of an organization or community. At any point in your career, you are either a thermostat or a thermometer. You either define the temperature of the people around you and help them achieve their goals and dreams, or you simply do as you're told and be a follower and never inspire. How do you become the thermostat?

Improve 1% each day in the areas of physical, emotional, mental, and spiritual health. This 1% compounds very quickly. Every day, do something to help the people around you achieve greater competence, better relationships, and more freedom in their choices. Repeat this: help others, then give them full credit. Whether it's your boss or your colleagues or your friends or family or whoever.

Bad employees and leaders do the opposite of the above. But leadership starts at the bottom, does these three things, and floats to the top.

In conclusion: Leadership is a vague term because sometimes the boss is not the leader. Sometimes his court rules the king. Sometimes the artist is supported and driven by the leaders in her entourage.

And there are so many pitfalls along the way. It's easy to get caught up in ego, money, bad visions, and the enticements that flirt with you the higher in the ladder you go. The feeling of, "Ok, I've done it!" when there's still a long path to travel on. So that's why I never trust the articles that say: "here's how to be a good leader". But I know that I have succumbed to all of the above pitfalls. And if I try to just avoid them (or do them LESS), then maybe one day I can be a good leader. A leader of what? Well, first, myself.

· · · · · ✳ · · · · ·

A Rich Employee Has an Evil Plan

You can't pin The Rich Employee down. He's not going to stay at his job forever (well, he might, but he or she has other stuff going on the side). He's going to help you but he's not dependent on you. There's always something cooking in the oven and probably in the toaster and on the grill as well.

Richard Branson made his first million or so with his music magazine. But did he stop there? No, he had an evil plan. Let's start a record label. Did he stop there? No, he had an evil plan. Let's build a galactic space empire. He's on it!

Every job I've ever had, I've had my eye peeled out for the next thing. Did this hurt my employers? Of course not! Often, the next thing allowed me to bring more value to my current thing. When I was busy starting my first web development business *while I was an employee* doing web development, I was learning tons of skills I wouldn't have had if I were just in it for the paycheck. When I was running a hedge fund, I had a chance to network and see hundreds of other hedge funds until I had so much knowledge of the business I was able to start a fund of hedge funds.

When I was writing books and publishing them through traditional publishers I learned so much about the publishing business that I basically built my own publishing company and started publishing through it.

I have to confess: although I love this concept of "Evil Plans", I highly recommend reading Hugh Macleod's book on the topic, titled, of course: "Evil Plans". The entire workforce can be divided into the people who have an evil plan and the people who don't and that division, I suspect, is very similar to the rich employee mindset, versus the poor employee mindset.

HOW A POOR EMPLOYEE THINKS

·············· ✳ ··············

T here's not much to say about "The Poor Employee" mindset.

Most people start with it. I had it for years. The reality is: there is a gap in income between "owners" (people who tie their financial success and well-being to the value they deliver) and the employees who have bartered freedom and growth for the mythological holy grail of the stable paycheck. As I mentioned, income is down versus inflation and yet the economy always returns to all-time highs. How can that be? Because in large cases, jobs that previously were done by employees are either outsourced more cheaply to other countries or are replaced altogether by technology.

Many people think that education will be a buffer that can help them prevent this happening to them. Not true. At first you needed a college degree. Then you needed a graduate degree to keep up. Now not even that helps, and even Google has said they will no longer look at degrees as a filter for determine if someone gets a job. Everything you learn in school can be outsourced to someone who learned it more cheaply or learned it more recently.

A great example is Scott Young, who decided he was going to get a 4-year education at MIT for just $2000. Normally a 4 year education at MIT would set you back about $300,000 in student loans at a 7% interest rate that even a bankruptcy can't get rid of. First they educate you, then they garnish your wages for the rest of your life and, god forbid you decide to be a painter or an entrepreneur they will just go into your bank account and take your money. Believe me, I've seen it happen. But MIT had videos for all of their courses online. So Scott Young bought all the books, kept up with the classes, took the tests, and got the education within 10 months. Did he get a piece of paper with his name on it and the words "Massachusetts Institute of Technology" sprawled lazily across the top in nice ostentatious calligraphy. No, he did not get that. Will some jobs penalize him because he did not spend $300,000 for that piece of paper? Yes, some jobs will penalize him for that. But those are exactly the jobs that will fire you once they figure out how to outsource you. They aren't looking for people with the "Rich Employee" mindset. They are looking for a factory worker, a cog in the machine that they know has a verified credential. All you are is a verified credential in those jobs and once they find a cheaper version of you, they will use it.

And yet Scott Young saved 3 years of his life, and $300,000 to get the exact same skills. During those extra three years he gifted to himself, he can learn many more skills, he can learn how to be innovative, how to sell, how to create and execute (things that no college teach) and he can leapfrog all his peers that are still stuck in the old mindset. And that explains the income inequality gap.

Note: I went to college. I even went to graduate school. In other books I describe what and why this was a horrible mistake and what the outcome of those mistakes were.

Some people say to me, "you wouldn't be writing these books and have had all of your opportunities if you had not gone to college." I don't know. I went to college in a different era. But also, I suggest reading my books where I describe my experiences of making use of my degree and what happened to see if it was really a positive or a negative. Also important to note: there are many ways to get educated now as opposed to 1986, my first year in college. I wish I had the advantages that kids have now. And you know what? I do have those advantages. I am in the middle of at least five online courses at any given moment. They are great, I learn a huge amount, and I'm able to choose what I want to learn, guaranteeing that I have a great chance of re-membering the courses afterwards.

The only way to avoid this income inequality gap is to avoid the Poor Em-ployee Mindset. i.e. these things

- Works for a paycheck
- Works 9-5
- Gossips
- Under promises, sometimes Over Delivers
- Doesn't understand the vision
- Tries to get credit
- Doesn't Have an Evil Plan
- Thinks "what can I get?"
- Spends time hating others for getting perks
- Complains about clients and co-workers
- Uses passive aggressive techniques to try to control outcomes
- Never invests in him or herself
- Uses money for showing off and status rather than learning new things
- Never comes up with great ideas
- Does only what is required to keep the salary coming
- Gets to work on time, or late, and leaves as early as possible
- Calls in sick on crucial days
- Shuffles papers to pretend to be working

- SURFS THE INTERNET OVER 50% OF THE TIME IN PURSUE OF PERSONAL INTERESTS
- CAN'T WAIT FOR WEEKENDS AND VACATION TIME OR HOLIDAYS
- ASKS FOR RAISES OFTEN AND WITHOUT ANY MERIT
- CREATES CONFLICT AND UN-EASE IN THE TEAM
- GETS DEPRESSED OFTEN
- HATES THE JOB

HOW TO BECOME A
RICH EMPLOYEE

.... ✳ ....

BECOMING A RICH EMPLOYEE IS A PRACTICE. YOU WILL
GET BETTER AS YOU APPLY THE PRINCIPLES IN THE
BOOK AND BUILD A DISCIPLINE AND A MIND-SET THAT
PREPARE YOU FOR IMMINENT SUCCESS.

THE RICH EMPLOYEE
MIRACLE MORNING

.... ✳ ....

Hal Elrod was dead for six minutes. The car he was driving crashed head on into a truck. His girlfriend, sitting next to him, was unscratched. The roof of the car sliced open his head, causing brain damage. Bones in his face, his arm, all over his body were broken and he was in a coma for six days (during which time his girlfriend broke up with him). When he woke from his coma the doctors told him he might never walk again.

You are the alchemist of your life. The universe, perfect for 14 billion years, has given you everything you need to thrive. And yet...we often want to forcibly change the universe to fit our own selfish needs. What idiots! I'm sure Hal did not want to hit that car. Did not want to be told he might not walk again. Did not want to go through years of therapy and misfortune as a result of this single event.

This is where alchemy comes in. We're all given this chance at some point in our lives. We're all given the tools to turn misfortune into gold. 15 years later Hal is a father, runs a successful business, and is a bestselling author of the book "The Miracle Morning". Along the way towards that he was also the top salesman at a $200 million in sales company. In other words, having a near-death experience transformed him into the Rich Employee mindset. Why I love to podcast is because I can just call Hal up and say "Can I talk to you about your book?" What a great scam podcasting is!

The universe is a contradiction. It is infinitely open and yet we can't escape it. It is 99.9999% empty and yet is filled with everything. Atoms bounce around totally randomly and yet defined by the most precise equations. Einstein said, "God doesn't roll dice" and yet...every moment is unpredictable. We'll never understand the contradiction and we shouldn't try. Trying has led to myths, to misconceptions, to wars, to anguish.

Hal didn't fight what the universe had dealt him. He turned the fear and the pain and crushed it down into a diamond. The diamond he now calls his "miracle morning" routine that he put together bit by bit to save his life. And now by he uses that same routine to save the lives of thousands of others. I like his routine because it fits perfectly into what I call "The daily practice" of choosing yourself: striving to improve every day 1% across physical, emotional, mental, and spiritual health.

Different parts of our brain are activated when we read facts as opposed to when we read poetry. Because facts we try to remember... and poetry we try to unravel a mystery of words mixed with art. We're so ignorant and lonely and overwhelmed by this vastness — this story that tells everything but reveals nothing. And yet we're all in it together.

What if every moment we turned the facts of our lives into poetry? To give up trying to assign meaning and turn all of our periods into question marks.

Doing these daily practices, or miracle morning routines, is how we begin to unravel that mystery. Maybe this one thing is the only thing I really believe in. The rest...I'm wide-eyed and just born and want to learn.

My grandfather used to say to me when I was little, "if the universe had an end, what's on the other side?" He'd keep repeating it, because we both were trying to figure it out. My brain hurt trying to think about it. Because there's no answer but it begs for one. I've never died like Hal. Maybe it's irrational but I'm kind of jealous of that he did. People who die have a story for the rest of their lives. This morning I'm going to get ready to die. And this morning that's how I'm going to live.

····· ✳ ·····

HAL ELROD'S MIRACLE MORNING STRATEGIES

REMEMBER THE ANAGRAM: S-A-V-E-R-S

"S" is for Silence

- MEDITATION
- PRAYER
- BREATHING

Whatever helps you start the day with calm thoughts.

"A" is for Affirmations

Encouraging words you tell yourself to achieve your goals, eliminate your fears, be healthy and happy, and live out your purpose. For example:

- TODAY I AM OPEN TO LEARN NEW THINGS
- TODAY I COMMIT TO NO GOSSIP
- TODAY I AM WRITING 10 IDEAS TO HELP OTHERS
- TODAY I AM A RICH EMPLOYEE BECAUSE I ADD VALUE TO OTHERS
- TODAY IS AN ADVENTURE
- TODAY I REFUSE TO PAY ATTENTION TO THE NEGATIVITY INSIDE, I LET IT GO
- TODAY I AM CONTENTED WITH WHATEVER LIFE BRINGS MY WAY, AND I WILL MAKE THE BEST OF IT
- TODAY I WILL WRITE A LIST OF PEOPLE I HELPED DURING THE DAY
- TODAY I WILL GIVE CREDIT TO MY BOSS AND THANK HER FOR THE OPPORTUNITY TO WORK HERE
- TODAY I WILL LEARN ONE THING ABOUT THE HISTORY OF THE COMPANY I WORK FOR

"V" is for Visualization

Imagine yourself doing each thing, step by step, that you need to achieve your goals. Then imagine what it will feel like when you succeed. Note: it's ok if goals change. They always do. The key here is to just get that feeling of accomplishment flowing through the body.

"E" is for Exercise

It doesn't matter if it's the gym, or 20 minutes of walking, or 10 minutes of anything. Just get the blood flowing in the morning.

"R" is for Reading

Read books that contain positive ideas and suggestions on how you can improve yourself. Learn the knowledge of the people who have done the things you want to do. They've spent a lifetime learning those things and now you can spend a week or a month learning them also (more or less) by reading their books. I've listed some in the resources chapter of this book.

"S" is for Scribing

Writing or journaling is a great way to clear out the mind, to get creative, to connect neurons, to take advantage of the fact that most people never exercise their idea muscle. At the very least, combining this with the Daily Practice I've recommended in my prior two books, you can write down your ten ideas a day here.

This is Hal Elrod's morning routine. I mention it here not because I do it (I do some of these things but not all) but because having a healthy morning routine, whatever it is, is important. This is a suggested one that has worked for Hal. When I write about my "Daily Practice" it's because it's worked for me. The right mindset leads to the right actions, but vice-versa also. You can't be stuck in your head all the time. You have to take actions and develop positive habits that start the second you wake up. You carry those habits with you into the day and everyone around you will notice.

HOW A RICH EMPLOYEE CREATES HIS OR HER SIDE HUSTLE

· · · · · · · · · · · · · · ✳ · · · · · · · · · · · · · · ·

I see a lot of books out there that say things like: "Use this company, put your buttons here, here is how to do SEO, here is where to put your shopping cart, etc." That's fine. Those books are very valuable.

Today.

But tomorrow the rules will change. The rules are changing every six months. I can give example after example about what works today but that may or may not help you tomorrow. What helps is getting the mindset of the Rich Employee. It might make you more successful at the job, it might make you successful at creating multiple sources of income, it might make you a "lifestyle entrepreneur" (your own business that is good enough to pay the bills) or it might make you a successful entrepreneur. Most people, though, have jobs. And to make the leap from job to entrepreneur is a difficult one. And often unnecessary.

For me, I stayed at my job for a full 18 months after I started my first business. How come? Because being an entrepreneur is not about creating risk for yourself, it's about mitigating risk. I didn't want to make a leap that could be catastrophic. Now...having a Poor Employee mindset is almost certain to be catastrophic. So I'm always looking for people who have created successful side businesses that ultimately bloomed into multiple sources of income for themselves. You can do this whether or not you are an employee, an entrepreneur, or anywhere in between. And what I look for is not the specific techniques, although I want to find that out as well, but one-step higher - the process or system for developing a side job.

This is where Mimi and Alex Ikonn come in. I think I'm in love with Mimi Ikonn. Oh, and also her husband Alex Ikonn. Don't want to confuse anyone! Mimi makes videos of her, delivers real value to people, and then makes over a million a year because of those videos. I don't know how old Mimi is. She's much younger than me. So Claudia and I asked Mimi and Alex if we could interview them because they also seemed very happy.

What they told us was a very simple way in which they made millions. I am absolutely sure the same techniques that worked for Mimi and Alex can work for anyone. As they were talking to me, I had them lay it out step by step as I took notes in my waiter's pad. These come from the notes:

A) EMOTIONS

Mimi became obsessed with beauty and hair. She and Alex watched before and after videos of women who were getting hair extensions.

"They seemed much happier after getting extensions," Alex said. "Whenever there are strong emotions about something you know there is an opportunity". So Mimi started making videos of herself discussing hair and beauty and hair products.

"I never thought I would get more than 1,000 views," Mimi said. "But I loved doing the videos. And I wanted to share my love for the topics with as many people as possible." Now she has had a quarter of a BILLION views on her videos with 2.7 million subscribers.

B) HUB AND SPOKE

People ask: "How do I get traffic to my blog". Or "how do I get buyers of my book." or "How do I get people to follow me on Twitter." A lot of it is about loneliness. We sit in our house writing blog posts and then hit Publish. We want family to love them. We want friends to love them. And then we want the world to love them. I'm really just talking about myself. I know when people enjoy things I do, I feel as if I have a family. I'm happy. Mimi loved making the videos but needed traffic.

So they did the only two-step technique that gets traffic online for anything you want to do. Well, make it a three-step technique. And again, the specifics are not so important. I have seen them change every single year for the past 20 years in a row. But the ideas have remained the same.

1) LOVE

Know more, love more, express more, bleed more, than anyone else. Was Mimi the only one doing videos on beauty and hair? No. But maybe she put more passion into it.

2) SPREAD THE LOVE

Alex would take images and posts and links to her videos and spread them on Pinterest, Instagram, blogs, other sites and have them all point back to her YouTube channel. I call this "the Hub and Spoke" approach. Youtube was the hub, with a dozen or so spokes reaching out to popular sites that all would link back to the hub. For you, it might not be YouTube. It might be your Facebook page, or a LinkedIn group you manage. Or a blog. Or Pinterest. Or whatever. Trust me it will change. But hub and spoke works. When I built stockpickr.com I was up to a million users almost instantly.

How come? Because I started writing articles for over ten different websites and would, throughout the articles, link back to stockpickr.com. I also guest blogged on various popular blogging sites and ultimately bloggers would write reviews of stockpickr. Same approach as Mimi and Alex took.

3) MAKE MORE LOVE

No matter what you do - some will be good and some will be bad. Not every video or post is going to have views. So you do more.

When you do more, several things happen:

A. More people find you.

B. You rank higher on search

C. You improve

D. People who find you start clicking on your older videos so now they start to get more views.

The "Make More Love" technique always works.

Michelle Phan did 54 YouTube videos before she made a massive hit.

Hugh Howey had already ten novels before he published "Wool" which became a massive bestseller. Clayton Christiansen applied for NASA for 18 years in a row before they accepted him. Make more love.

C) 1000 PEOPLE

Note she said she only thought she was going to get 1000 viewers. The number 1000 keeps coming up with people who have HUGE audiences.

Kevin Kelly wrote about this in a great post called "1000 True Fans". He writes about it on kk.org. He also talks about it on my podcast. Tim Ferriss talks about how every one of his posts he makes sure he's going to deliver value to at least 1000 people. Of course he delivers much more value than that. But 1000 seems to be the right number that people who know seem to focus on. Keep focusing on delivering value for a 1000 and then they tell 2 friends and so on and next thing you know you have a quarter of a billion views, five bestsellers, movies being made about you, you go into space, your own makeup lines, and on and on and on, depending on what it is you love.

D) BUY LOW, SELL HIGH

Alex and Mimi noticed that many of the other beauty videos were talking about a specific brand of hair extensions for women. So they went to my favorite place in the world - the mall.

"We saw these products were priced at $500," Alex said. "So then we went on Ali Baba and saw the same products being sold for $100. We then went to the manufacturers and saw we could buy directly for $50. The exact same products that were being sold for $500." They borrowed from mom. Borrowed their full amount off of their credit cards. And they placed an order. Then, I imagine (they did not tell me this) they prayed. By the way, this works for almost every product. Why do people go to stores and buy name-brand products for $100 when they might have been built for only $5. That's a huge gap. The gap is filled by advertising. People like brands they recognize and are willing to pay up for it. Will that gap decrease? I'm not sure. We are inundated with up to 2500 advertising messages a day. The advertising industry is a trillion dollar industry. There's money there because it works. It gets people to buy more than they normally would.

At sites like AliExpress you can buy name-brand cameras, for instance, for $100 and then re-sell them a second later on Ebay for $400. Or why even buy them first. Sell them first and then buy them and ship directly to the Ebay buyer. This is called drop shipping and many people use it to create their side gig.

E) SOFT SELL

Mimi talks about many products on her videos. She expressed a radiant, confident personality and talks about everything she is wearing, what her habits are, what products she uses. She *never* sells anything. But underneath the video is just a link: www.luxyhair.com. The orders came in one at a time. Then 100 at a time. They sold out of their inventory, paid everyone back, and bought more. In their very first year (2010) they had over a million in revenues. Ever since then they've had more than a million a year in profits. Never once using the words "buy this" anywhere.

F) QVC-A

The most successful people have a model for their success. I think that's why I enjoy Peter Thiel's "Zero to One" book so much. Or Peter Diamandis's: "Bold". Or Marcus Lemonis's TV show: "The Profit".

Each book has a different, but very simple model for how to achieve success or how to judge which companies are successful. Mimi and Alex developed their own model, they stick with it, and have used this simple model to keep jumping from success to success. Alex explained it to me:

Q - *Quality*

Everything they do is quality. The cameras they use for videos ("But not overdoing it, because this is YouTube and not television," said Mimi). The setting they use and how it fits their message. The products, etc.

V - *Value*

Mimi is not trying to sell anything in her videos. She explains what she does and how she does it. She does the research and believes in the products. Rather than asking, she is giving. "When you give a billion dollars in value," Alex said, "you get a billion dollars or more back."

C - *Consistency*

I read a book about television once by TV mega-executive Grant Tinker. He was Mary Tyler Moore's husband, ran NBC for awhile, and then ran MTM productions producing such shows as "The Mary Tyler Moore Show", "Bon Newhart", and a dozen other super hit TV shows. I only remember one thing in the book. He said: "Whenever they changed the time or date of a show, then that show would die. If you moved a show from Tuesday at 8pm to Thursday at 8:30pm then you just lost your whole audience."

Mimi said, "if you are going to put out a video once a week, put it out once a week. Put it out the same day each week if you can. Don't do once a month. Don't do random. Your audience starts to anticipate and look forward to your shows and knows when to expect them."

A - *Authenticity*

Mimi only talks on the videos about what she believes in. There's no fluff. There's no pitch. She's exuberant and it shows on each video.

H) LESS

Mimi and Alex were working 80-100 hour weeks. They had the money in the bank. They had achieved their goals. They loved what they were doing but when you hit a lifelong goal you start to ask, "is that it?"

They got depressed.

Goals are a myth. Our ancestors for 200,000 years didn't have goals. Every day started from scratch: hunt, forage, eat, sex, sleep, and wake up to a new day. Then we were told to find our "goals". And now everyone asks, "I'm 17 years old and feel like I've accomplished nothing in life. What should I do?" Learning to find happiness with less is true wealth. Claudia and I recently got rid of most of our belongings, for instance. Then we started cancelling most meetings that I had set up. Sometimes it was hard. I had agreed to an event and then I would cancel. Ultimately we are the sum of our experiences and not the sum of our belongings. There is nothing wrong with making money but it is only one small part of living a life of comfort, of compassion, of calm.

Mimi and Alex started to focus more on the other things that were important in their lives. "And you know what happened?" Alex said. "The more we did that, the more money we made."

· · · · · · · · · · · · · · ✳ · · · · · · · · · · · · · · ·

I am always curious how people made money through a channel like YouTube or any channel for that matter. I think their technique can easily be replicated (perhaps with a little trial-and-error but that is the case with any endeavor you are going to take seriously). I'm afraid I don't have a face for YouTube. Or Instagram. And I'm not even sure I have a face for podcasting. But I think I love doing what I do. And I like having the time to explore other interests and ideas. And then sometimes I like doing nothing at all. There's nothing wrong with that.

HOW DOES A RICH EMPLOYEE HANDLE WHEN OTHERS GET JEALOUS AND TRASH HER OR HIM?

················ ✴ ················

I t's a sure thing that as you become a rich employee and gain momentum in your success others will hate it. It is not a question of "if" it is a question of "when" because it is guaranteed to happen. People either grow with you or prefer to stay at their comfortable lower level and hate you.

I've had four death threats. I've had several major media outlets write articles trashing me (with hundreds of comments agreeing. Even two rap songs composed just to bash me).

I've had people even show up unexpectedly at my house ready to argue with me. Maybe the worst was exactly four years ago today. I wrote an article on July 4 on why I was against all wars. I don't know enough to have a real opinion. All I know is that there is nothing that I would ever feel strongly enough about where I would allow my 16 year old daughter to take a gun to another country and shoot other little kids.

That's what war is. That's what all wars have been. The history books with the justifications get written later.

I was afraid to publish the article anywhere. So I went to a website devoted to yoga. I figured, "All of these people will love me." Because I wanted to be loved. There were about 500 comments to the article. Maybe more. One person wrote: "you're worse than Hitler." Others were saying, "you are the worst scum of the Earth." And it wasn't just strangers. After a few months I realized one of my best friends wasn't calling me back. Finally I got ahold of him. I said, "what's going on?"

He said, "I read that article. You must be for slavery."

I said, "We've known each other 20 years. Why didn't you pick up the phone and just ask me? Of course I am not for slavery or anything even remotely close to that."

But he said, "Let's just wish each other well and not speak anymore."

Another time I wrote an article about my family. I wrote about my father and my fears of how I was making the same mistakes he made in life. The article was about my own fears.

My sister wrote me and said she would sue me unless I took it down. She said, "I never want to speak to you again for the rest of my life." So now I haven't spoken to one of my best friends, or my sister (who had really been my best friend all my life) in years.

A few days ago, someone wrote me and said I was probably the dumbest person alive. I get those at least once a day. Two days ago it was more like ten emails saying that. It's very painful to get hate mail. From friends or even from people you don't know or from relatives. No matter who it is. I don't like it. So I had to learn to deal with it. Here's how:

A) Live Life Like it's your Last Day

This doesn't mean, "Ok! Eat cake! Party all day!"

This means, when I see my wife, or my friends, or my children, or people who I love, it may be the last time I see them or speak to them.

Will I spend those moments agonizing about people who hate me, people stuck in my head shouting at me in my imagination?

Or will I give the people I love my full attention. Because I will miss them. Because nothing is better than being around people you love.

It's my choice always in those moments and I know exactly what I will choose.

B) This Too Shall Pass

Whenever there is "outrage porn" directed in my attention I learned one rule: if I don't deal with it for 24 hours then it goes away.

If I respond to one hateful comment. Or one outrageous statement against me. Or one completely insane outburst, then I have to restart the clock and it's another 24 hours.

For those people, it's just a game of reaction-reaction.

I'd rather play games I enjoy.

C) They are Junk Status Binging

When someone lashes out at me, I quickly realized what was happening, as painful as it was at the moment.

They were afraid.

I only know this because I look at when I get angry at something. It's usually not because what the other person did. It's usually because they said or did something that triggered some fear inside of me.

My fear of not being liked. My fear of losing some status. My fear that if I lose status maybe once again I will l go broke, or lose my marriage, or go homeless, or start drinking and taking drugs. Or whatever has happened to me in the past that gives fuel to my own fears.

I don't like fears that are touched. So I clothe it in the armor of anger and I lash out.

And that's what other people do. To me, to you, to everyone. We are all victims on both sides of this.

Sometimes the most confident-seeming people are the ones who are most afraid, the ones with the most armor surrounding them, the ones who need to be cradled the most but prevent that by lashing out at those around them.

When someone is afraid and angry like that, they want to feel they are better than you. So without earning that "better" status (whatever that might mean), they try to get status over you by trashing you.

This is similar to "eating our fears" when we binge on junk food. Ultimately, we are tribal animals, and all mammals earn their rank in the tribe and know very well where they sit on that ranking.

With outrage porn, it gives people a chance to think they can move up or down in status by junk-trashing you.

And when I get offended by it, I also have to be aware of the same thing. They are dealing with their fears but I'm also dealing with mine.

So now I say, "thank you". Because it is ONLY in those moments where I can relax and release and let go. These are the moments we are given to spiritually grow.

D) HAVE A VISION

Every day I get emails from people who are in pain. People who feel stuck in life. Stuck in their careers. Stuck in their passions or their relationships.

Or even worse, lost and perhaps suicidal. People who were climbing a ladder and for a moment, at least, have lost their grip in the dark and don't know how to find it again.

I've been on that ladder many times. I've also lost my grip. I've fallen all the way down.

I like to think that I want to help. But I don't know if that's possible. You can't tell people how to find light when the room is pitch black.

All I can do is tell what works for me. How I have gotten back onto that ladder and kept climbing. What practices and methods have worked for me that I have to stick to every day, or else.

I never write to hurt anyone. I only tell what happens to me. I never give advice. I only say what has worked for me.

When you write and work from the heart, from your own personal vision that is your safety net.

Don't go from your safety net into someone else's spider web. They will poison you and then suck the blood out of you.

Ultimately, we are a single drop of water that is dropped into the middle of a deep ocean.

What happens to that single drop of water then? It disperses throughout the ocean, rippling to all shores. If the ocean is your safety net, no storm can rock you for long.

E) COMEDY

Laughter cures all. Laughter is a very primal sound we make. It is older than human language – perhaps millions of years older.

What does it signify? It signifies that there was danger, but now the danger is over. There is relief. There is joy. There is celebration.

And yes, there are fart jokes.

When I feel my body reacting to someone else's opinion of me (I feel it in my chest, my stomach, my head), and I want to react, I want to argue, I want to make the call and find out why, who, when, WHY – I watch comedy.

I laugh. It's ok. This is more important for my survival than arguing. And, in fact, medically that's true also. Anger will cause stress, inflammation, heart attacks, and strokes.

Laughter has been demonstrated to be life healing. It's an inner massage of the body.

And given all of our choices in our short lives, while we are all trapped here together spinning through space at 4000 miles a second until we flame out into a mist of nothingness, what would you rather do — laugh or cry?

·············· ✳ ··············

People say, "it's none of my business what other people think of me". This is one of those statements that are both *true* and *not-true*. Intellectually it seems true.

But we're not all intellectuals. Sometimes we feel that animal urge to respond, to react, to cry, to be in pain.

So this is all a practice. A practice for growth. And the people who lash out with their opinions about us are our greatest teachers.

Sometimes it feels horrible. But running a marathon is hard. Flying through space on a tiny planet is so hard it's a miracle.

Don't waste the miracle living inside other people's fears. Be the drop of water that disperses through the infinitely wide ocean.

And, in the worst case, listen to fart jokes a lot.

HABITS OF THE MENTALLY
STRONG RICH EMPLOYEE

·············· ✳ ··············

When I was a kid I used to skip school, hide behind my house until my parents left, and then go off to play chess with John Nash. Not THE John Nash, the Nobel Prize winner who also had schizophrenia, but his son, who was then a very strong player. We would go over to his house (where his father and mother also lived) and play all day and then I would go home before my parents got home from work. The son also had schizophrenia and I sort of could tell but we focused our days on playing chess. At the time, I didn't know who his father was. This was a family of brilliant people. His son was a strong chess master. The father was a Nobel Prize winner. Maybe that makes them mentally strong, maybe not. One time John and I went to play in a father-son tournament. We had to pretend he was my father so we could win. Later on, I didn't tell my own father about it. Again, not the best qualities of mentally strong people.

John, the son, disappeared and we lost touch. I last saw him I think in 1988. Since then I've met a lot of incredibly brilliant people. Because of my podcast and businesses I've been involved in I've met some of the smartest people, some of the most successful people, some of the most brilliant people in the world. Maybe they are mentally strong, maybe not. Often many of us are very good at constructing masks and it is never really known what is deep inside of us. What we keep hidden for fear of death if others were to find out. But I can tell you what is most common with some of the people I have encountered and maybe then you can tell me if you think these are qualities of mentally strong people. I would like to know.

All of these things anyone can do. Anyone can learn to be mentally strong and change the world as a result. Whenever I did not cultivate these attributes, I quickly was on my way towards developing "The Poor Employee" mindset. Whenever I worked on these, I increased my chances for success. I'm not quoting a scientific study. This is just my experience.

A) RELATIONSHIPS

The mentally strong people I know, the ones who have achieved the most in life, have ALL had incredibly strong relationships: Friends, spouses, partners, and so on. I've interviewed billionaires, well known movie directors, athletes, scientists, artists. All have believed in the saying "you are the average of the five people you spend your time with". If you build up strong relationships, it means they are supporting your ideas, adding to them, helping you execute them, and not constantly fighting you or dragging you down.

B) HONESTY

This is not religious but math. The brain takes up 2% of the body's mass and burns up 25% of the body's calories each day. One in four calories you eat goes to fuel your brain. When you lie, one side of your brain has to deal with one set of lies. And the other side of the brain has to deal with the other set of lies.

So to be at optimal mental strength you now need twice as many calories. This is impossible. The best way to be mentally strong is to be honest so all of the fuel in your body can be used efficiently at propelling your brain from strength to strength instead of fighting off the attacks on your weaknesses.

C) It's Not About Me, It's About You

Whenever a girl broke up with me, it never seemed to be about me. That's ok. That was a line to make me feel better. I guess I should be grateful for the many people who tried to make me feel better by blaming themselves. But true mentally strong people constantly are focused on others. They are solving problems for other people. They don't think, "How can I make money?" since money is just pieces of paper fueled by a mythological story. They think, "What are problems in the world that I can solve?"

They think, for instance, healthcare is a mess. And since we all know "prevention is the cure", how can I develop a product that helps with prevention and diagnostics. And, if you were a genius like Elizabeth Holmes, you would drop out of Stanford, make a company called Theranos, and do exactly that. That is just one example. Mentally strong people are always solving other people's problems. The problems of the individual get solved as a byproduct of solving the problems of the many.

D) Reading

I've interviewed over 150 people now for my podcast. Here is one question nobody ever hesitates on: What are the last books you've read? Do you know why mentally strong people read? I have my guess. We all have one life to live. But when you read, you get to absorb the curated life of another person in just a few days. So if you read a lot, your one brain can hold onto the critical points of potentially thousands of other incredible people. You can bathe in their lives and come out a stronger you.

I asked Freeway Rick Ross, the largest drug dealer ever, what books he read in prison that turned around his life. He couldn't read or write before prison. But then he taught himself. He told me instantly: *"As A Man Thinketh"*, *"The*

Richest Man in Babylon", and *"Think and Grow Rich"*.

I asked Tim Ferriss, author of The Four Hour Work Week. He said, "Radical Acceptance", "Essentialism", and "The Effective Executive". All 150 people I have interviewed gave answers instantly. I have no doubt if I ask them again next week they will all have different answers. I have never met a mentally strong person who wasn't a voracious reader.

E) HEALTH

Because the brain burns so many calories, you have to have health in other areas of your life. It's hard to be mentally strong, to be creative, to execute, to change the world, if you are sick in bed. This is not being judgmental towards those sick in bed. Sometimes we just get sick. We can't help it. But almost everyone I've ever dealt with in business or in life who has gone on to greater and great successes all acknowledged the importance of constant healthy transformation of their bodies.

This doesn't mean lift 500 pounds. It means sleep eight hours a day. It means eat well (which simply means: less on processed foods, more on vegetables, and exchange your 15 inch plates for 10 inch plates), and move. Movement doesn't mean running a marathon. It might just mean walking a lot. Our paleo ancestors got their exercise from walking and climbing on their daily hunt for food. This kept them healthy enough to be our ancestors so I thank them every day for that by following their model.

F) CURIOSITY

If you are talking to someone and they say something interesting but you don't understand, do you interrupt them and ask them what they mean? I often don't. And then what happens? Then, for the rest of my life, I will never understand what they mean. Sometimes I'm afraid to ask questions because I don't want to seem stupid or I don't want someone to be annoyed at me or I'm feeling shy. The only way to learn new things is to ask questions and be curious. Find the people who inspire your curiosity because those are the ones you will most learn from. Then ask them questions. The more stupid you feel asking a question, the more you HAVE to ask the question. If you feel shy asking one question, then ask TWO questions. Every mentally strong person has this one thing in common: the things they most remember that has changed their lives have been the answers to questions they asked. If they never asked those questions, their lives would not have changed.

G) Learn, Say, Repeat

We think we learn in school. We take a class and a brilliant professor gives a lecture and we supposedly leave the class smarter. But here is the science. Within 45 minutes of leaving a class, college students have already forgotten 80% of what was said in the class. By the next day, they have forgotten just about 100%. Here's how to remember: First you hear something. If it interests you, write it down as a note (carry a notebook. I carry a waiter's pad because they are cheap). Then use it in a conversation within an hour. Then use it in a conversation the next day and then the next. NOW there is a decent chance you have learned it. Because you build various connections in your brain that have now been programmed with that nugget of information. That's how learning takes place. Mentally strong people learn how to learn.

H) The Idea Muscle

Try this: come up with 10 ideas for surprises for your spouse's next anniversary, or a nephew, or someone you care for. The first three are easy. But, for me, then it gets harder, and by #7 I'm counting the list over and over again to see if I reached 10. Ideas are a muscle that needs to be exercised. If you get hit by a bike and are stuck in bed for two weeks recovering, then when you leave the bed your leg muscles are so atrophied you need therapy to walk again. The same thing happens with the idea muscle. It needs to be exercised every day or it will atrophy. How do you exercise it? Pick a theme, any theme will do, and write down ten ideas a day. Every day.

When I was broke and suicidal and scared, I started doing this. My life has changed 100% every six months since then. It's been incredible. Like magic. I wrote this and shared this with others. Now I get emails from people every six months telling me how their lives have changed also.

When I was interviewing the rapper Coolio he told me he wrote lyrics down every day for 17 years before he had his first hit. A year after his first hit he had the best selling song on the entire planet. When he described that song to me he explained which elements and from which musicians who came before he, he meshed together to create his hit.

This is called "idea sex". When you are an expert in one category and an expert in another then you are the greatest in the world at the intersection. Exercising the idea muscle, plus learning, plus idea sex, will make you be the best in the world at whatever you aim.

What about execution? Execution ideas are just a subset of regular ideas. If you have an idea you want to execute on, then your idea list the next day should be, "What are the ten next steps I need to take?" Should you then take them? I don't know. Mentally strong people probably make those lists 100 times a year and only need to execute on one of them to change the world. Give yourself permission to have bad ideas. It's only through diligent mining of the universe inside of you that you find the gems that will light up the world.

I) PERMISSION

Mentally strong people give themselves permission. Why did the Google guys come up with the 8th search engine and think theirs was special? Why did Elizabeth Holmes think it was fine to drop out of the best school in the country to pursue a business dream? Why did Henry Ford, after failing twice at car companies, think it was a good idea to start a third car company? Why did the Wright Brothers think it was ok to make a plane with spare parts from their bicycle shop when the government was spending tens of millions? They all gave themselves permission to do something that has never been done before. They all gave themselves permission to have many bad ideas. They all gave themselves permission to risk their reputation and the forked tongues of the people who would fight them. They gave themselves permission to slip and fall and get up and dust themselves off and try again. And again. And again. And again. They gave themselves permission to love something so strongly that every neuron on their brain would light up and conspire to make their dreams come true.

If you don't give yourself *permission* to create a new world, chances are nobody else will.

J) PRESENCE

I regret so many things from my past. Maybe that one time I lost all of my money, I could've used it to help my father live a little bit longer. Maybe I could've held onto my house. Maybe I could've been smarter about business. Most of the time I am anxious. Will I give a good speech? Will this business I invest in work out? I hope it does. I don't want to go broke again. But whenever you regret the past, or are anxious about the future, you are time traveling. Time traveling seems exciting but it isn't. You can time travel all your life and then suddenly you are dead without ever having lived in the present moment, the only moment that exists.

Whenever mentally strong people notice they are time traveling they take a step back. They say, "What can I do right now to help others?" instead of wasting time regretting the past or worrying about the future. Worry and regret never solve tomorrow's problems and only drain away energy from today. Presence will always solve this moment's problems. Mentally strong people solve problems, love people, are curious, stay healthy, have idea sex, are honest with you, and make the world a better place.

K) Life Changes Fast

Don't hang on to it. Just go where it takes you. Don't try to control it. As Ice-T told me during an interview: "Ride it, don't guide it".

The Universe just spent 13.8 billion years creating you. There's nothing you can do to try to control it. Don't try to have a single career. To have a "purpose". To "figure out what you want to do". Just do the best you can each day. If you don't know what that means, you have to figure that out for yourself. If anybody tells you what it means, then they don't know what it means.

L) Experiences are More Valuable Than Goods

Don't buy goods. Don't buy a house. Don't buy a fancy anything. Buy (or have) good experiences.

This is how neurochemicals work. You have 4 or 5 that make you happy (oxytocin, dopamine, etc.). They get into your brain, they trigger happiness, and they metabolize very quickly so the happiness goes away and you need more. When you buy something nice, the neurochemicals spike, and then go away. When you have an experience, you have days (or months) of anticipation for the experience. Then you have the experience. Then you have the memories that can last forever.

That's a lot of happy chemicals all the time bursting through your head. If you just use this one rule, you'll have a happy life.

M) Listen

You already know all the words in your head. You only get something new if you listen to the words that are coming out of someone else's head. Always look to add to who you are instead of subtract. When you talk you subtract. When you listen, you add.

N) Pretend Everyone is Going To Die Tomorrow

If I knew tomorrow I was going to die then I would eat cake all day today. Do this instead: Live life like it's the last day for EVERYONE ELSE. Imagine now you see someone. You know it's their last day but *they don't*. So you will treat them really well and feel compassion for them. And then they will treat you well. What a nice virtuous cycle, one that helps everyone and makes you happy. Oh, and it's ok to eat cake sometimes. Eat what your heart wants.

O) Politics, Government, News is Completely Uninmportant

Congress makes minor laws that lobbyists bribe them for. But you can make a child happy. And Google is making cars that drive by themselves. And writers write poetry, and painters make beautiful art. Do something stupid and ridiculous that you love. Do something today that tomorrow people will say is great. The news will never do that. Art and innovation will. We still remember art from 3000 years ago. But we don't remember what laws passed that day. Or what the Kardashians were doing.

P) The 5 x 5 Rule

A. You're the average of the 5 people you spend time with.

B. You're the average of the 5 thoughts you most have .

C. You're the average of the 5 types of food you eat.

D. You're the average of the 5 things you are most grateful for.

E. You are the average of the 5 things you are reading today.

Q) Autonomy

Always take the job, pursue the life, and have the friends that allow you to have as much freedom as possible. I asked Nassim Taleb on my podcast what job should one have. He said, "night watchman, because nobody is around to bother you and you can pursue all your dreams on the side."

R) Food Sleep Move

Every cell in our body changes every seven years. What are the cells made out of? The food you eat. I've seen this happen with my own eyes. I watched someone who only eats good foods and never eat junk. Over the past 7 years she has developed a glow. She stands out in a crowd. It doesn't matter what you look like. If you eat well (and you know what that means) then you will get that glow. Sleep: we know one basic thing: at night when we are tired our brains are not that productive. So what do we do? We sleep. Don't fall for "sleep porn" — that the less sleep you have, the more productive you'll be. It's the reverse.

Sleep rejuvenates the brain. If you sleep 8 hours instead of 2 then your brain is 100x more productive during it's peak time of the day (about 2 hours after you wake up. That 100x compounds into amazing.

And movement. Your body depends on oxygen circulating. It circulates better when you move. Walk 20 hours a week. I do all of the above. And every six months my life changes so drastically I can hardly believe it.

HABITS OF THE POOR EMPLOYEE

·············· ✳ ··············

THE POOR EMPLOYEE HAS AN OPINION

W hat opinion can you possibly have? Global warming? Ok, good luck changing the world. War? Ok, good luck stopping the $200 billion defense lobbying industry from having war. She/He should treat me better! Again...good luck. People say to me, "if everyone thought like you then the world would be a mess." Oh really? I have one word to say back (which breaks my later statement about defending myself):

"Manure".

In the 1890's horses, carrying people to work, dropped 4.5 million tons of manure on the streets of Manhattan, *every year*. That was the big environmental problem of the day. "NYC will be buried in horse manure by 1950!" screamed the headlines. It doesn't matter what your opinion about this was. None of the people living in NY solved the problem despite the 1000s of opinions. People with passion for mechanics in Detroit made something called a car. Problem solved. Do what YOU love to do today. Surrender the results. The more you surrender, the more results there will be. The way you solve the world's problems is to solve your problems. Then trust.

······ ✳ ·····

THE POOR EMPLOYEE THINKS THERE IS SOMETHING DPECIAL S/HE IS HERE TO DO

You realize there are 8.7 million different species on the planet. Do you think the trillions of members of all of them were put on this Earth with a special purpose? Like they have to be an opera singer. Or solve a hard math problem? There's 1000 different species (species, not individual organisms, which are around 10,000,000) living on your body right now. 80 in your mouth. So you better shut up. The last part of our body to evolve was the pre-frontal cortex, which allows us to adapt to different environments. No other species has one. This let us move from hot Africa to cold Alaska and every place in between. But is also the part of our body that makes us think we have a special purpose. Our own unique, little, private purpose which will win us awards and acclaim and make us feel better. It won't. But I understand you feel that way if you are young.

So here's the solution and it works and can be applied at any age: get good at three, four, or five things. Then find the intersection. Then become the best in the world at the intersection. That's how you can pretend to do your special purpose. When I say "get good" it doesn't mean 10,000 hours of practice with intent. Maybe it means 1000 hours. Or even less. Then if you get good at 5 things you're now the only one in the world who has put 1000s of hours into the intersection. Now you're the best in the world at that.

· · · · · · ❋ · · · · ·

THE POOR EMPLOYEE TALKS A LOT

You really don't have to talk as much as you do. The average human says 10,000 words a day. Maybe cut that in half. Or say nothing. I tried saying nothing for a whole day the other day. It's hard. But it felt like magic when I finally spoke again. I valued every word that came out of my mouth. But try to talk less when you're young and know nothing. Like when you're 19 years old and you want to talk about the status of your relationship. There is no status. You're 19. Guess what. Even if you're 50 you don't need to talk about it. Treat the other person nice. Then your status will be good. If you hit the person you are living with then your status won't be good. Talking won't do anything. This holds for most things. Listen to me. Or better yet, just listen.

······ ✳ ······

The Poor Employee has No Career

The average person has 14 careers. And that number is probably going up.

My careers have been: academia, computer programmer, writer, "web series creator", CEO of a web design company, day trader, hedge fund manager, writer about finance, venture capitalist, book writer, speaker, internet entrepreneur (made a website that got popular), deal maker, self-improvement blogger and book writer, podcaster, and a few more I'd rather not say because they are either horribly embarrassing or might get me into legal trouble. Young people say, "I don't know what I want to do when I grow up." Or "I want to be a doctor". These two statements have a 99% chance of being wrong. I got an email a few weeks ago: "I'm a nurse and I have $210,000 in student loan debt and now I don't even want to be a nurse. What should I do?" I don't know. You're probably screwed.

····· ✳ ·····

The Poor Employee Thinks it Needs X to Get Y

- "I need to look good (or have a good job), to meet a boyfriend/girlfriend."
- "I need to have a million dollars before I can

WRITE A NOVEL AND RELAX".

- "I NEED TO GO TO TRAVEL THE WORLD TO GET LIFE EXPERIENCE."
- "I NEED TO DO WHAT MY PARENTS SAY."
- "I NEED TO GO TO GO A GYM TO GET HEALTHY".

Here's the reality that many people don't get. There are many paths to that mysterious "Y". Don't assume you know what they are. I told my daughter something the other day. I said: "you know that quote I always tell you?"

She said: "Ugh. Yes, 'There's always a good reason and a real reason.'"

"Ok, I'm going to tell you another one:

'There's always a back door.' "

"What does that even mean?" she said. We were walking around Washington Square Park. She was looking with envy at all the college students walking around. I think she wants to be one.

"It's ok if you don't know what it means," I said. "I can't explain it. Just don't assume the front door is the only way to enter something you want."

Right now Snoop Dogg is saying he wants to be the CEO of Twitter. That's never going to happen. But he can say it can. And then maybe it will. Who knows?

I'm sure he's said 1000 ridiculous things in his life. And you know what? 1% of them have happened and have created an amazing life for him. The rest of us don't say any of these ridiculous things. So nothing ridiculous and amazing happens to us.

······ ✳ ·····

The Poor Employee Thinks: If I Don't Do This Then Bad Things Will Happen

- "If I don't go to college I can't get a job"
- "If I don't get a house, I won't have roots. I'll waste money on rent."
- "If I don't have money, I won't be able to buy anything. People won't like me."

Society is very powerful. We get 2500 media messages a day telling us our Do's and our Don'ts. All 2500 of those messages are wrong. How do I know? Because people wouldn't have to pay to show you those messages if they are right. They know the messages are wrong so they pay to put them in front of you. If you believe the messages then you would think you can join the army, and either A) choose to go to war or B) go hiking and learn computer programming at the same time. You can't.

Don't let the media messages program your brain.

Don't let the media messages predict the future. Because it's a fake future.

······ ✳ ·····

The Poor Employee Thinks, "I Can't Leave."

Young people think they can't leave. How many times did I spend an extra year in a relationship, or a city, or a job, or a school, because I was afraid to leave? Afraid I had the power to truly hurt someone with my decision. You can get up and leave right now if you are not happy or if you want to do something new.

THE POOR EMPLOYEE THINKS S/HE HAS TO DEFEND THEIR POINT OF VIEW

In the next 60 years, a lot of people are going to hate you. In fact, the more people you try to help, the more people will hate you. I don't know why this rule exists but it does. For every ten people you help, one person will hate you. And you will want to defend, explain, argue, or respond back. You can't change their mind. They are going to hate you no matter what. They are going to try and get in your head so you wake up thinking about them. Delete them. Delete their comments, their emails, their connections to you, any contact you have with them. You can't change them. You can change YOU to not care. The more haters you have, it means you will have 10 times the number of people who love you but are silent. When they offend, don't defend.

Remember one thing: You are the coach of your future self. You are the only coach of your future self. Everything that happens in your future is a direct result of what you do today. I've made a lot of money and lost it miserably and got scared and depressed and cheated and ran and hurt and cried and was suicidal.

None of that helped my future self. Here's what did, when I was at my lowest and darkest moments. When I had the pills right in front of me. When my kids were asleep in their bedrooms and the night kept ticking away in my brain, refusing to let me sleep, refusing to stop my heart from racing in panic. I took a walk every day. I stopped dealing with the people whom I felt bad around. This was very painful to me. But better that than dying. Or defending. I spent more time with the people whom I felt good to be around. I started reading every day. 40% of people who graduate college never read a book again. If you are in the remaining 60% you are 1000x ahead of everyone else.

I started writing down 10 ideas a day. Then I started sending ideas to people, without expectation back, with the hopes that the ideas would help people. I forced myself to practice being grateful for everything I had. Two arms. Two daughters. A friend, then two friends. Then three. The more grateful you are, the more you attract things to be grateful for. And by doing so, all the mistakes I made in my youth started to change.

HOW THE RICH
EMPLOYEE LEARNS
A RICH EMPLOYEE IS ALWAYS LEARNING

· · · · · · · · · · · · · · ✴ · · · · · · · · · · · · · · ·

Someone stole $90 million from a company I was involved in. I'm a poor judge of people. Some things I can't learn. I tend to like people too much. So it's hard for me to be a good judge of people, no matter how much I try. So I find other people who are good at judging people and I ask them to help me.

Don't force yourself to learn something if you don't want to or it's not a natural talent. What's the role of talent? Very small. But you have to start with it. Talent is the seed of skill. How do you know if you are talented? If you loved it when you were ten years old, if you dream about it. if you like to read about it. Read the below and you'll know what you are talented at.

Trust me when I say: everyone is talented at many things. In the past 20 years I've wanted to learn how to do some things really well: writing, programming, business skills (leadership, sales, negotiating, decision-making), comedy, and games.

So I developed a ten ten-step technique for learning.

A) LOVE IT

If you can't start with "love" then everyone who does love will beat everyone who "likes" or "hates". This is a rule of the universe. The first humans who crossed the arctic tundra from Siberia to Alaska in -60 degree temperatures had to love it. The rest stayed in the East Africa Savannah. The very first day I wrote a "Hello, World" computer program I dreamed about computers. I woke up at 4 am to get back to the "computer lab" and make even bigger programs. When I first started to write every day, I would write all day. I couldn't stop. And all I wanted to talk about with people were different authors. When I was 10 years old I wrote a gossip column about all my fellow 5th graders. I read every Judy Blume book. I read everything I could. I loved it. Most of my friends got bored with me and soon I was very lonely. Except when I was writing.

READ IT

Bobby Fischer wasn't that good at chess. He had talent but nobody thought much of him. So around the age of 12-13 he disappeared for a year. He did this later in his 20s. But at 13 when he came back on the scene he was suddenly the best chess player in the US, won the US championship, and became the youngest grandmaster in the world. How did he do it? He barely played at all during his year of wandering.

Instead he did two things:

A. He studied every game played in the prior century. In the 1800s.

When he came back on the scene he was known for playing all of these antiquated openings but he had improvements in each one. Nobody can could figure out how to defeat these improvements. In fact, the final game of the World Championship many years later, in 1972 when he was playing Spassky, he brought out his 1800s arsenal to become World Champion. Spassky desperately needed to win to keep the match going. Fischer needed to draw to win the title. Spassky started with a very modern attacking opening ("The Sicilian"). But then around 13 moves in, all of the commentators watching gasped. Fischer had subtly changed the opening into an old-fashioned very dark 1800s opening called "The Scotch Game". Spassky didn't have a chance after that.

B. He learned enough Russian to read the Russian chess magazines. At the time, the top 20 players in the world were all Russian. The Americans didn't really have a chance. So Fischer would study the Russian games while all of the Americans were sitting around with openings and styles the Russians already knew how to defeat.

Consequently, when Fischer competed in the US championship in the early 1960s it was the first complete shutout, all wins and not a single draw. Studying the history, studying the best players, is the key to being the best player. Even if you started off with average talent.

· · · · · · ✳ · · · · ·

TRY IT. BUT NOT TOO HARD

If you want to be a writer, or a businessman, or a programmer, you have to write a lot, start a lot of businesses, and program a lot of programs. Things go wrong. This is why quantity is more important than quality at first. The learning curve that we all travel is not built by accomplishments. It's only built by quantity. If you see something 1000 times, you'll see more than the person who sees the same thing only ten times. Don't forget the important rule: the secret of happiness is not "being great" - the secret is "growth". If you only "try" you'll get to a level that is natural for you. But growth will stop and you won't be happy.

· · · · · · ✳ · · · · ·

Get a Teacher (Plus the 10x Rule)

If I try to learn Spanish on my own, I get nowhere. But when I go out (and now marry) someone who is from Argentina, I learn more Spanish. With chess, writing, programming, business, I always find someone better than me, and I set a time each week to ask them tons of questions, have them give me assignments, look over my mistakes and tell me where I am wrong. For everything you love, find a teacher and that makes you learn 10x faster. In fact, everything I put on this list, makes you learn 10x faster. So if you do everything on this list you will learn 10 to the 10th power faster than anyone else. That's how you become great at something.

· · · · · · ✳ · · · · ·

Study The History, Study The Present

If you want to learn how to be a GREAT programmer, not just good enough to program an app application, but good enough to be GREAT, study machine language. Study 1s and 0s. Study the history of the computer, learn how to make an operating system, and Fortran, Cobol, Pascal, Lisp, C, C++, all the way through the modern languages of Python, etc.

If you want to write better, read great books from the 1800s. Read Heming-way and Virginia Woolf and the Beats, and the works that have withstood the test of time versus millions of other books, and they have, for a reason. They are the best in the world. Then study the current criticism of those books to see what you have missed. This is just as important as the initial reading.

If you want to study business, read biographies of Rockefeller, Carnegie, the first exchange in Amsterdam, the junk-bond boom, the 90s1990s, the financial bust. Every depression, all the businesses that flourished in every depression.

Read "Zero to One" by Peter Thiel. Watch "The Profit" on CNBC. Read about Steve Jobs. Read about the downfall of Kodak in "The End of Power".

Don't read self-help business books. They are nothing. You are about to enter a great field, the field of innovation that has created modern society. Don't read the average books that came out last year. Step up your game and read about the people and inventions that changed the world into what it is today. Read how Henry Ford had to start three car companies to get it right and why "three" was the important number for him. Read about why Ray Kroc's technique for franchising created the world's largest restaurant chain. Read how Coca-Cola makes absolutely nothing, but is the largest drink company in the world. Write down the things you learn from each reading.

······ ✳ ·····

DO EASY PROJECTS FIRST

Tony Robbins told me about when he was scared to death on his first major teaching job. He had to teach a bunch of Marines how to improve their sharpshooting. "I had never shot a gun in my life," he said. He studied quite a bit from professionals, but then he came up with a technique that resulted in the best scores of any sharpshooting class before then. He brought the target closer. He put it just five feet from them. They all shot bull's-eyes. Then he moved it back bit by bit until it was the standard distance. They were still shooting bull's-eyes.

Richard Branson started a magazine before he started an airline. Bill Gates wrote BASIC before his team wrote Windows.

E. L. James (and yes, I'm including her) wrote Twilight fan fiction, before she wrote "50 Shades of Grey".

Ernest Hemingway never thought he could write a novel. So he wrote dozens of short stories.

Programmers write "Hello, World" programs before they make their search engines.

Many chess grandmasters recommend you study the endgame first in chess (when there are few pieces left on the board) before you study the other parts of the game.

This gets you confidence, it teaches subtleties, it gives you greater feelings of growth and improvement — all steps on the path to success.

· · · · · · ✳ · · · · ·

STUDY WHAT YOU DID

The other day I threw everything out. Everything. I threw out all my books (donated). I threw out all my clothes. I threw out old computers. I threw out plates I never used. I threw out sheets I would never have guests for. I threw out furniture (four book cases) and my TV and old papers and everything. I wanted to clean up. And I did. I found a novel I wrote in 1991. 24 years ago. It was horrible. For the first time in those 24 years, I re-read it. I studied what I did wrong (character un-relatable. Plot too obvious. Deus *ex machina* all over the place).

Someone told me a story about Amy Schumer, one of my favorite comedians. She videotapes all her performances. Then she goes back to her room and studies the performance second by second. "I should have paused another quarter-second here," she might say. She wants to be the best at comedy. She studies her every performance.

When I play chess, if I lose, I run the game into the computer. I look at every move, what the computer suggests as better, I think about what I was thinking when I made the bad move, and so on. A business I was recently invested in fell apart. It was painful for me. But I had to look at it and see what was wrong. Where did I make a mistake. At every level I went back and wrote what happened and where I might have helped better and what I missed. If you aren't obsessed with your mistakes then you don't love the field enough to get better. You ask lousy questions: "Why am I no good?" Instead of good questions: "What did I do wrong and how can I improve?" When you consistently ask good questions about your own work, you become better than the people who freeze themselves with lousy questions. Example: I hate watching myself after a TV appearance. I have never done it. So I will never get better at that.

······ ✳ ·····

YOU ARE THE AVERAGE OF THE
FIVE PEOPLE AROUND YOU

Look at every literary, art, and business scene. People seldom get better as individuals. They get better as groups.

The Beats: Jack Kerouac, Allen Ginsberg, William Burroughs and a dozen others.

The programmers: Steve Jobs, Bill Gates, Ted Leonsis, Paul Allen, Steve

Wozniak and a dozen others all came out of the Homebrew Club.

The art scene in the 1950s: Jasper Johns, De Kooning, Pollack, etc. All lived on the SAME STREET in downtown NYC.

YouTube, LinkedIn, Tesla, Palantir, and to some extent Facebook, and a dozen other companies came out of the so-called "PayPal mafia".

All of these people could've tinkered by themselves. But humans are tribal mammals. We need to work with groups to improve.

Find the best group, spend as much time with them, and as a "scene" you become THE scene. You each challenge each other, compete with each other, love each other's work, become envious of each other, and ultimately take turns surpassing each other.

······ ✳ ·····

DO IT A LOT

What you do every day matters much more than what you do once in awhile. I had a friend who wanted to get better at painting. But she thought she had to be in Paris, with all the conditions right. She never made it to Paris. Now she sits in a cubicle under fluorescent lights, filling out paperwork all day.

Write every day, network every day, play every day, live healthy every day. Measure your life in the number of times you do things. When you die: are you two writing sessions old? Or are you 50,000?

······ ✳ ······

FIND YOUR EVIL PLAN

Eventually the student passes the master. The first hedge fund manager I worked for now hates me. I started my own fund and his fund went out of business.

But how?

After all of the above, you find your unique voice. And when you speak in that voice, the world hears something it has never heard before. Your old teachers and friends might not want to hear that voice. But if you continue to be around people who love and respect you, then they will encourage that new voice. There's that saying, "there are no new ideas." But there are. There are all the ideas in the past combined with the new beautiful you. Now it's your turn to teach, to mentor, to create, to innovate, and to change the world.

FREQUENT AND IMPORTANT QUESTIONS RICH EMPLOYEES HAVE

HOW DOES A RICH EMPLOYEE DEAL WITH A CRAPPY BOSS WHILE IN TRANSITION?

·············· ✳ ··············

My boss wanted to publicly humiliate me. He came into my office with a bunch of my colleagues. I was very busy playing chess online but I could see he was serious so I clicked away that window and stood up.

"Did you release the newest version product to the client last night?" he asked. The client was Pfizer. The product was software that automatically translated Pfizer technical manuals from English to about five other languages. I wrote the code.

"Yeah," I said, "like you said I had to or we would be late on our delivery."

"Well, the client called," he said, "and they found a bug."

My colleagues were nodding their heads. One of them must have been called by the client who then proceeded to take out his life's troubles on her by screaming at her on the phone so she then complained to my boss who was about to take out the fact that he really wanted to beat his wife but I was a convenient second place.

"Ok," I said.

"So you released a product to the client that had a bug in it," he said.

"Uhh, yeah, I guess," I said.

"Let me get this straight. You mean to tell me you released this without triple-checking every possibility?" he said.

"Well, I double-checked but I did not triple-check," I said.

"Are you making a joke? This is a very serious issue. You NEVER EVER RELEASE A PRODUCT WITHOUT TRIPLE-CHECKING." His face was red. Everyone was watching.

"Ok," I said.

"Ok what?" he said.

"Ok," I said. "I QUIT."

Which felt great because just 10 minutes earlier I had gotten off the phone with Rob Martin at HBO who had offered me a job with almost a 50% salary increase (from $28k to $40k) plus $2k in moving expenses.

"Well," the boss (now "Chris" because he was no longer my boss), "you don't have to quit. It was just a mistake."

"No," I said, "I don't like when people yell at me. You shouldn't do that to people. I quit."

Chris looked at me for a second. I think all of my colleagues had their jaws slack and wide open in that Monica Lewinsky way where the whole world could just explode any moment.

"C'mon man," Chris said, "I was just concerned about the client. But I'm more concerned about whether or not you are happy in the workplace. No hard feelings."

"That's ok," I said, "I don't ever like being yelled at. So when people yell at me, I quit. You know as well as I do that every bug can't be checked. You should treat people better. Now," and I shrugged my shoulders for affect, "I give two weeks notice."

I never told him I just had gotten an offer. A few months later he had a question about my code and he called about it and I told him I forgot the code completely and couldn't help him. About six years later when I was running a venture capital firm he called, "hey buddy," and he said he had a business to pitch me. I called him back and left a message. "Super excited to hear about your business. Send me a detailed business plan with description, bios, projections for the next ten years, a passcode to unlock an online demo, you know, all the usual things." And he did. He put a lot of work into it. I never called him back. He left repeated messages for about two months. He called my secretary and said he would stay on the phone until I picked up but I never did. I was really immature back then.

Bosses suck. I've had some real good bosses (hi Tom!) but mostly really bad bosses. Fortunately, before you finally quit there's some good ways to deal with them and train them.

Remember BAD BOSSES ARE DOGS and needed to be treated that way. Here's very important advice on dealing with a DOG that happens to be your BOSS.

A) Never Kiss Ass:

Then your DOG knows he can keep stretching the boundaries until you're on the leash and not him. Never stop by his office just to chat. Never do any brown-nosing. This is the rule from "How to Deal with Crappy People". If your boss is a crappy person then you want to engage as little as possible. Only work stuff. Never joking around. Never anything that builds a meaningful dialogue that he will twist later. Don't make friends with an animal. This is not every boss. Just crappy bosses.

B) Never Talk Badly Behind His/Her Back:

He will eventually hear. He will also sense it. DOGS are psychic. When you don't talk badly behind his back his natural suspicions will lessen about you and he will treat you better. Talking badly behind his back is a passive way of engaging with him and this goes against rule "A" above.

C) Always Give Him/Her Credit For Everything:

DOGS like to be loved. When you do work and give him full credit then the result could be: promotions for him, which leads to promotions and salary increases for you. Never begrudge when he takes credit for something you did. Everybody already knows it was you. I once had a boss who was promoted to a high level position. Everyone stopped by my desk to congratulate me because they knew the reasons my boss were promoted for.

D) Write a Cover-Your-Ass Memo Every Day Describing What You Are up to and Who You are Dealing With:

You need to do this every day: what you do, who you speak to, etc. so that all blame gets deflected off you. Nothing can stick. When I was running Reset (which made websites and software for Fortune 500 companies) every project manager working for me had to do a cover-your-ass summary to the client of everything they did the day before. Every detail had to be tracked.

E) Build Relationships With His Network of Colleagues and Contacts

Eventually your boss is going to try to screw with you. But s/he can't get away with it if your network includes her or his *entire* network. This isn't as hard as it sounds. If your boss deals with someone then it's not hard to ask her or him for coffee so you can "learn more about their job so you can help them better." Nobody will say "no" to that and everyone will be grateful when you start helping.

F) Help Other Employees of Your Boss with Their Jobs

Do this without acknowledging at all your feelings about the boss. They are going to want to vent to you. Remember rule "B" above. Don't let them vent to you. It's none of your business what their work problems are. This is very important. But help them with their jobs so that when it comes time for everyone to start pointing the finger then you're the last person they point to.

G) Over Deliver

On anything he asks you to do provide an extra touch. This is how he gets promoted. When you are more creative than him, over deliver for him, and he gets full credit. Then he gets promoted. Then you get promoted.

H) WHAT'S YOUR MARKET VALUE?

You know that BS phrase "Always be selling?" It's sort of true: Always be Selling Yourself! Always be applying for new jobs for two reasons. The job market is like any other market: prices are ruled by supply and demand. So you always want to know your market value. Information is power. The second reason is that it gives you a good plan B if you need to leave. Ideally you leave before you leave. i.e. freelance and generate multiple streams of income so you know you can afford to quit.

G) THEN QUIT

Corporate America is almost by definition an exploitative environment. They pay you less then they make from your services. So you have to make sure that if you are going to let them get away with it then they can't take advantage of you and that if they treat you badly you have other options.

Why Is It Especially Important For Women Rich Employees to Become Idea Machines?

·············· ❋ ··············

C laudia writing here, getting into James's book shamelessly just for this chapter, but an important one!

We are at a point in history where we have to stop pretending we are not brilliant beings. We, women, need to become idea machines, pronto. The power that comes through this simple exercise of writing 10, better and better ideas every day, is a gift we owe to the world. We have to own our talent and admit that we have something to bring to the table. We are in a magnificent position to affect change in the world in a feminine way. There is no winning in playing small anymore.

I said that recently during a podcast interview. And of course, in true "Idea Machine style" that conversation invited me to elaborate and come up with ten/eleven reasons why it is so important for women (and men, of course) but specifically, in this case, for women, to become idea machines. Here they are:

1) Women Still Get Paid Less Than Men

Ideas are the currency of the 21st century as James has been saying for years, which is true, because the old job and the retirement, or even social security is rather "iffy" at best these days. We don't exactly know *how* the money will come when we start giving away our best ideas freely, but then again, in the past we also didn't exactly know, because if we did then we were at a "job", where the number was small and fixed. Nobody ever generates wealth that way because there is little value added at a fixed, "boring" job.

Thinking of wealth in terms of ideas levels the playing field. Just like the Philharmonic orchestra got more women into their pool of talented musicians once they started auditioning by hearing the musicians play BUT with a screen covering their likeness and gender. *Great ideas* are the screen through which we level the playing field. Once the screen of good ideas is up, we add so much value that respect ensues, regardless of gender, ethnicity, background, or any other prejudice.

2) LET'S ASK MORE QUESTIONS

I'll tell you one thing that disheartened me while reading Sheryl Samberg's *Lean In*. She says that when she gives talks it is always men that raise their hands and ask questions. Women rarely ask. I am not saying we should be COO's, or start companies, or run Facebook's, and I am also NOT saying we should be more like men. NO.

I am just saying we need to start raising our hand and speaking up and asking questions. In the book "The Confidence Code" (see recommended reading below) I read that studies show that women will apply for a job (or ask a question) only if they feel 100% prepared.

At a recent conference I decided to make an experiment. Instead of asking a question as I always do now, I thought I would keep quiet and see what would happen, I was specifically looking for the behavior of women in the room. Would they ask questions? Not a single woman brought her hand up to ask a question. Not one. There were plenty of opportunities. Men, on the other hand, literally jumped off their chairs in an almost foolish fashion, and raised their hands so high it looked like they were waving at someone a mile away in a train platform.

Now, just to clarify, women *did* ask some questions but only when we were broken into groups of 30 people or less, not when the entire hall of 250 people was watching. It was the men that asked all the questions then.

Men apply for a job if they feel they are 70% prepared! And ask a question even when they don't have one as I witnessed in my mini-experiment at that conference. This is something I've been sensing quite a bit, and that is why these days I ASK QUESTIONS. Every time. Even if I don't know what I am about to ask.

Just as I did in a previous conference where, in another experiment, I asked lots of questions. One time as I lifted my hand I had no idea what I was going to ask. But I did have a question, and the question came to me between the moment I raised my hand and the moment the speaker looked at me and said: Yes?

It is evolutionary for us to raise our hands, to ask, to take risks, to be bold. Because otherwise our voice is missing from the conversation.

We live in a time in which little girls get shot in the face because they want to learn how to read and write. This is why I feel it is important for me, as a woman who gets to live in a place of relative peace, to participate, to get involved, to Lean in.

And the questions can and might be bad at first, that is OK, it is all a practice. Just like listing ten ideas a day gets the idea muscle ready, flexible, and in good shape, asking without knowing, just for the sheer thrill of participation will eventually teach us to ask better questions, to look for answers, to clarify what we didn't understand, and to lose the fear of being ridiculed.

3) THE TRANSFORMATION IS DECEIVINGLY SLOW BUT POWERFULLY POTENT

Some people have began listing ideas together with me since the book launch, and many are sharing them (sometimes daily in Twitter) I heard of someone who sent 10 ideas to a music festival, and now that festival invited him to help them with their crowdsourcing efforts. I sent 10 ideas to 99Designs because I used their services three times in three months and I had enough experience to know where they could improve.

The CEO wrote me a letter that week which is below, *typos and all*, so you can tell is real, he is probably a busy guy:

> *Hi. I'm the CEO of 99designs and I just wanted to let you know that we really appreciate your thoughtful feedback. We actioning items immediately that we can address around better communication/messaging and we are actively recruiting additional customer support representatives to ensure that everyone sees a chat window when needed (peak times sometimes makes chat unavailable to some users).*
>
> *Are you happy with your final design for your book cover? Is there anything else that I could do for you? Really happy to help in anyway and thanks again for the tough love... We are always striving to get better and feedback like yours helps make that possible. Kind regards.*

We then had some follow up conversations, and I thanked him for listening. He told me that he was going to talk to his staff and share the list with them. Now, the point of this is to show how it is *deceivingly slow*.

You may say me: "C'mon, a letter is nothing, that is not *money!*". And you would be right. But this is the way the world works these days. We send ideas, we add "real, actionable, and good value" to others and, it starts with a thank you letter it may continue with an invitation to come over and talk to the staff (as it happened to James with Amazon where they flew him to Seattle -twice) and then, just like that, relationships are built, you meet new people, you get new ideas, you get BETTER ideas. We don't need to see the end result; we just need to list ten ideas today. It compounds fast.

For example James got his book "Choose Yourself", and his most recent book "The Choose Yourself Guide To Wealth" in hard cover (which Amazon *never* does for self-published authors as of yet) — Because he is constantly sending them good ideas.

That is how the "POWERFULLY POTENT" part happens... it is compounding, not a straight line. It is nothing that you would "expect". It is an endless, giggly, upward spiral. That is the shape of the trajectory that transforms good ideas and participation into money -today.

4) Getting Out of Depression

Last summer I went to Thailand and I was suffering from one of those bursts of depression I get often. I was shocked when, after taking my pulse, Paul Dallaghan gave me a pranayama prescription that encouraged more solar breathing (right nostril) I don't want to go into details on that because I believe a prescription is that, something personal, but I did see the "RESULTS" We as women are more "receptive, lunar, open to communication, wanting to be liked" and on and on. Not all of us, of course. I don't want to generalize. And I know some women have a lot of sun energy in them. I am just saying that as per ME, and in my own experience, my feminine energy is more earth while men's is more sky.

In my case, I need to activate the more active part of my brain. Especially when I feel depressed. It is all nice for me to write my morning pages, journal and do collages, but The 10 ideas a day engage my mind in a completely different way. It gets me going in a way that is foreign to my basic nature of silent receptivity.

Listing 10 ideas per day connects me with the "how can I help?" energy in a more practical, go-get-it, sun way.

And as you probably have noticed, turning dust into gold is nothing compared to changing our energies from thinking: "all of this sucks!" to "how can I help", because that is graduate level alchemy. That is real and powerful transformation. We get unstuck via being healthy in all areas of life, taking care of ourselves, and listing 10 ideas a day.

5) Remembering To Give To Ourselves

When coming up with ten ideas a day we will have days in which it's simply impossible. Life is incredibly difficult, and things happen. As women we tend to want to help, soothe, and give.

This is a wonderful feminine quality but it is also important to remember that our own soothing, helping, and giving to ourselves is critical. So we may skip a day of doing the ten ideas if the world goes upside down. But we can take it again the next morning because our ideas are important. And because our contribution, the way we see the world, our thoughts, translated through a fine-tuned intuition of ideas is important.

Whenever I find myself upset I immediately think of listing 10 things I could do. I start with the most ridiculous ideas (because there are no ridiculous ideas, they are just ideas, I don't judge). It is usually through those that

I give myself permission to actually get out some pretty good ones. Remember: ideas can save lives. Ideas can save our stressed out days. Ideas can save relationships. Ideas can help us, and everyone around us.

6) CONFIDENCE

This is a tricky one for us women. There is an imbalance in how we are perceived weather we admit it or not. A Harvard study had two groups of women take a math test. The first group had to identify their GENDER before the test, the second one had to identify their ETHNICITY There were Asian women in both as I understand. Guess what group did better?

The one that identified themselves as "Asian" rather than "women", because "Asian women are good at math". We all know that, right?

These stereotypes DO EXIST. Denying them does no favors. Acknowledging them is better because then at least we know what we are dealing with. How does that play out in "confidence"? Let's see, have you ever had an idea and expressed it and then later someone else (perhaps a man) took it and used it as if it was his? This happened to me not once, but many times. I find it to be my responsibility to point out that that was MY idea, not because I want to be 'better than' but to reassure MYSELF, to regain my own sense of self-confidence.

The last time this happened to me it was with a well known marketer. We were having breakfast with him, James and me, and he just repeated my idea, took it and made it his own. I listened in disbelief, I think I even made a face gesture which went totally unnoticed. Then I slowly but surely clarified that I was the one that had said that *exact same thing* five minutes ago. It was awkward, it was uncomfortable, and it was unusual. Did I care? No! It's time I own my talent. Enough of letting things slip as if nothing.

I find that coming up with ten ideas a day gives me the confidence necessary to trust the words that come out of my mouth. By the way, this does not mean I turn into a mean person. If I say something that is out of line I still can acknowledge I was wrong. I am wrong many times and I have no problem saying I am sorry, but being an idea machine helps me identify when I am sure, in my bones, that what I am saying is the right thing and when you have that kind of confidence, when you know that something is the right thing for you, in your soul, then nobody can stop you.

7) What is My Passion? For Today?

I laugh when I hear people in Quora ask: "How can I know what my life purpose is"? Nobody can know that. Since I was born I have had at least 8 different "lives". There is no way that at 15 I could've said: "I will be a writer" forever. It just does not work that way. I am currently a podcast host, and author, the co-owner of a fast growing company, an executive producer of events, a video producer, a blogger, a yoga teacher, an idea machine and on and on. And with the idea machine, the PURPOSE changes every six months or so because as we start coming with lists of what we are interested on our lives change.

When we pay attention to what is igniting our inner fire, then life has no evolutionary choice but to lead us in the direction of what we feel passionate about... TODAY.

8) Cutting Ourselves Some Slack

Last week I overheard a beautiful young woman with four kids say that she does not push herself enough. She had just finished practicing two hours of yoga asana. I HAD to ask her: "Do you hear yourself speak?"

I was not mean, I was encouraging. I think any woman with four kids is a super hero period. So, speaking of cutting ourselves some slack., let's remember that most of the time we do everything that men do, feel all the same stresses, and still make the bed and cook breakfast, thank you very much. Ideas help us recognize our brainpower, our dedication, our power of transformation, and the results we bring into the world. And if you are ever in need of some padding in the back do this:

List your "I DID LIST" for today

List all the things you DID, TODAY

You WILL BE SHOCKED. Guaranteed.

9) WHEN THINGS FALL APART

When things fall apart, as they do, having a toned idea muscle allows the wisdom of the feminine energy to change perspective, to notice where our strength lies. Heck! We are showing up for our daily practice! It helps us to reassure ourselves that this, too, shall pass. And there is nothing like going '10-idea's on a problem... Because it shows different ways of looking at it, and in doing so we shift our perception.

10) THERE IS NO BEAUTY IN PLAYING SMALL

I am married to a strong man and I can see what happens when I play as if I am less, or not as important, and also, what happens when I act from my full power, as an equal, and sometimes even as a wise-teacher. It is much more productive and leading to peace and balance when I stand in the fire-center of my power and own it.

For example, yesterday I had a great business idea. I was not invested in it, but I liked it, so I was toying with it. I told James about it and he said it would not be necessary because the company we are running is already bringing in money. This bothered me for some reason, but I could not get my finger into why.

After some reflection I realized that in James's saying that, what I actually heard was: "you don't have to". So I told James: "Honey, when I speak up about an idea, how about if you encourage me, rather than tell me that I don't have to"? He immediately understood. Then he went to take a shower. When he came back he said he did not mean to put my idea down, but he understood how it could have that effect on me. Then he told me it was a great idea and he had ideas for me to make it better. Will I act on it? I don't know, but I certainly feel a lot better that I could improve on the idea a lot further and make it bigger with his help, rather than leaving it at "you don't have to".

And it made my relationship with James deeper. It is in conversations like this that I feel like a true partner, like the strong woman I know I am.

When I trust the words that come out of my mouth and yet have the humility to recognize that I don't necessarily know everything then I am playing to my strengths. I am honoring the feminine wisdom in me, the power bestowed upon me by being a female.

I am not a genius, but as a female I am as powerful -if not more sometimes-than the male energy. My energy as female is needed in the world, badly. And if we don't return to nurturing this part of our energy, if we don't bring to the front the feminine energy that births wisdom then we are doomed. This is the time for all of us as women to bring our voices to the front, to speak up, to let our ideas count, and to do what we know we have to do.

171

We can elevate the conversation. We can bring it up a notch, from silly gossip to what really counts, to how can we own our power? How can we be more honest with ourselves? How can we help each other, woman to woman (and men too, I love men) How can we make sure when a woman is interrupted, that we say "excuse me, I would like for her to finish her thought". How can we be more kind to one another? How can we get out of the way of our feminine wisdom?

11) FUNNY

A few weeks ago I got another of those bursts of depression. I bought an audio book... Ellen... "Seriously I'm Kidding". It made me feel better.

We women are GREAT at a sense of humor because we have to. I noticed one thing listening to Ellen, she has a phrase going somewhere and suddenly it will turn crazy, for example: she will say:

No woman is perfect... Except for Penelope Cruz

There is always that twist, that funny turn. I've never laughed more than when in a group of women who trust each other. We are witty people. This is why I am recommending the book (audio better really), because we can bring our brilliant sense of humor to the world too. One list I am going to be doing is "sentences that end in a funny twist" For example:

Amy Schumer: "I went to LA last week... Have you ever had your self esteem lowered?"

See the "twist"? We are great at it, and you KNOW IT !

RECOMMENDED READING

- LEAN IN
- SERIOUSLY I'M KIDDING
- BECOME AN IDEA MACHINE
- THE CONFIDENCE CODE
- BOLD

JUST ONE THING TO DO

·············· ✳ ··············

C laudia discovered the secret of the ONE THING. Not me. I hope she's not angry I'm writing about it instead of her.

When you discover something, it's normal to want to be the first to write about it. I don't blame her.

But, like with anything: there are many ways to, I don't know, "skin a cat"? Is that the expression? Why are so many people skinning cats?

Maybe it should be: there are many ways to slice a pie. I had a piece of pie yesterday. Peach pie. I guess I'm having trouble with this paleo thing.

Claudia raises her hand.

She went to one conference and sat on her hands and noticed not a single woman raised their hands but plenty of men did.

Here's what happened. Most of the men asked stupid questions. But some of the men asked good questions.
The reason women don't raise their hand (Claudia's theory) is that they are more afraid than men that they will ask dumb questions.

The next conference she went to, as soon as it was time for the audience to ask questions, she raised her hand .

"When I raised my hand, I didn't even know what I would say. I just raised it and figured I would come up with a question."

She raised her hand so much people started laughing and she would always be called on and she asked good questions. She stood out.

I have a hard time raising my hand. I'm afraid to talk at dinners. I have to push myself to speak loud enough to be heard.

So this story applies to me also. And I'm sure, many men.

She told this story at a recent event I spoke at. I spoke right after her. It's hard to follow her in a talk.

Guess what? Every woman raised her hand with questions. They raised them super fast. Great questions. I loved them.

I find that more women than men believe in things like the "Law of Attraction".

Actually, I know this to be true. When we went to a conference that featured "Law of Attraction" authors, it was almost all women in the audience.

We went to that conference because the conference organizers were publishing a book we were writing.
With the Law of Attraction, you don't have to raise your hand. You just have to think of things.

What a burden to raise your hand and ask when you can just think! The Law of Attraction is just chains to keep people's hands by their side.

You can only make a difference in your life when you stand out. When you aren't afraid to go beyond the fringe.

This is the place where both fools and geniuses live. I never know which one I will be every time I go there. But I hope I never forget the maze of pathways to get there.

All day long, all of us try to tell our inner story. We wear masks, we do dances, we hope that the story we tell matches the story of who we really are.

- IT'S SCARY TO HAVE ALL EYES LOOK AT YOU.
- IT'S SCARY TO NOT KNOW WHAT'S GOING TO HAPPEN NEXT. TO MAYBE BECOME THE FOOL.
- IT'S SCARY TO TELL THE STORY OF WHO YOU REALLY ARE AND LET PEOPLE SEE IT.

Raise your hand, hold it out until it's grasped from above and you are pulled up.

Carried over the drowning sea of heads, too afraid to tell their stories, too scared to breathe, until eventually they just sink to the bottom of their history, their stories left untold forever.

HOW DOES A RICH EMPLOYEE
MASTER NEW SKILLS?

·············· ✳ ··············

Are you satisfied with your life? Do you go to work knowing you could do better? Knowing there are unique talents in you that could make you great, the best in the world? This chapter is about achieving mastery. But also why it's ok to not get mastery in the traditional sense. You can define it, not use the definitions provided by everyone else. In other words, it's fine to be a loser.

There are a lot of books written on this topic. If you want to read an entire book on it, read Robert Greene's "Mastery" (or listen to my podcast with him). There's also "Outliers" by Malcom Gladwell. But it's not that hard. For one thing, most of us, and I mean me, will not be masters at anything. I try. I tried with chess. I hit the rank of "master" but that doesn't mean anything. I'll never be world class at it. I've tried with writing. I've been writing for twenty or so years. But I've known a lot of people who are among the best in the world in their field. I've read all the books. I've talked to all the people and dissected what they thought led them to their mastery. I've built and sold businesses to people who were masters of their fields in every industry. I've invested in people who were masters in their fields. So I've at least recognized who were masters and what they did. Take this then with a grain of salt but based on my experience and the experiences of all the people I've interacted with here are the elements of mastery. I also have some good news and bad news.

A) TALENT

I hate to say it, but talent is a factor. There's a myth that everyone is talented at least one thing and you just have to find it. This isn't true. Most people are not talented at anything. Most people can be pretty good at something. For instance, Tim Ferris shows in "The Four Hour Chef" how you can be a pretty good chef with four hours worth of work. I've tried his techniques and in four hours I made some pretty good dishes. Thank you, Tim. But at the launch of Tim's book he held a dinner where each course (I think there were eight of them) was cooked by a different chef. One of the chefs was (approximately) eight years old and his dish might've been the best served. That kid will be a master one day if he isn't already. That's talent.

When my chess ranking was peaking back in 1997 I played in a tournament against a girl fittingly named Irina Krush. She really did crush me in about 25 moves. After the game she told me, "May be your bishop to B4 move felt a little weak to me." She was right. She was 13 years old. I stopped playing chess in tournaments right that moment and now only play when I'm on the phone with people. She had talent. She's now one of the youngest women grandmasters in the world.

B) HOW DO YOU FIND WHAT YOU ARE TALENTED AT?

I think there are roughly two methods.

i) Take out a pad.

List everything you enjoyed doing from the ages of six to eighteen, before your life was ruled by college, relationships, crappy jobs, mortgages, kids, responsibilities, self-loathing, etc. I was talking to Lewis Howes on my podcast. He mentioned he always wanted to be an athlete since he was a little kid. He also mentioned that he used networking skills to help himself out even at an early age in order to deal with what seemed like poor academic skills. He found his two talents and became masters at both. Often, it's a combination of sub-talents that make you uniquely a master in that one field. For me, I don't know if I will master anything, but since I was a kid I loved writing, games, and anything to do with business. Maybe one day.

ii) Go to the bookstore.

Find a topic you would be willing to read 500 books on. If you can't wait to read all 500 books in the knitting section then you probably have a talent at knitting. Note that it is really ok to not be talented at anything. We weren't put on this Earth to be talented at knitting. Do you know why we were put in this Earth? I hope you know, because then you could tell me. But chances are there really isn't any reason.

We are ultimately a combination of all of our experiences, all of the things we are interested in, all of the things we flirt with. And that combination might look like garbage to everyone else. So play with your garbage and be happy. If you can do that, you're in the top 0.00001%.

C) Four Hours a Day

It's not a mystery Tim Ferriss's books all start with "The Four Hour..." I ask almost every master I encounter, in every field, how much time per day do they spend mastering their field. They did not give the standard Silicon Valley BS Entrepreneur answer: "I work 20 hours a day and if I didn't need to sleep I'd work 30 hours a day". You can't get good at something if you are working 20 hours a day. In fact, something is very wrong in your life if that is how much you are working at ONE thing.

The typical answer is: "I study four hours a day". Anatoly Karpov, former World Chess Champion, said the maximum he would study chess is three hours a day. That's a guy who was a world champion. Then, when he wasn't in tournaments, he'd spend the rest of the day exercising, studying languages, doing other things to balance out his life.

D) History

In any area of life you want to succeed at, you have to study the history. All art is created in context. If someone wrote Beethoven's Fifth Symphony right now it would be laughed at. It wouldn't fit the current context of music, even though it would be a work of genius.

Andy Warhol tried many different areas of art before he decided that painting Campbell's Soup Cans were the right art for the right moment in time.

In any sport, studying the history of how previous world champions played and trained is critical towards figuring how you can improve on that training and playing. In any business, studying the history of that industry, the biographies of the prior executives, the successes and failures of those who went before you, is critical for mastering that business. For example, I had Greg Zuckerman on the podcast talking about the current resurgence in oil drilling in the US. Everyone thought the US was out of oil back in the 1970s. Well, now the fastest growing city in the United States is Williston, North Dakota and the US will probably be a net energy exporter by 2020. This is not a political opinion on fracking. It's just the reality of what is happening now.

If I were remotely interested in fracking I'd study where all the oil was drilled back in the 1920s, 1950s, 1970s. How the first wildcatters found their wells. What technologies were used. What's the history of the technology, how were improvements made, what's the history of the geopolitics around oil drilling. And so on. Somewhere in there is a path to getting incredibly wealthy. Not for me, because I couldn't care less about oil, but for someone. Or many.

E) STUDY YOUR FAILURES.

I was talking to poker champ Ylon Schwartz. He's won over $7mm in tournaments and untold millions in informal cash games. We grew up together playing chess until he made the switch first to backgammon and then poker. I asked him why a lot of people play poker for 20 years but never get better. What's the story? He said: "Everyone wants to blame someone. They want to blame bad luck. Or they had a fight with their wife. Or something. But the key is you have to study your failures. You have to take notes about your losing hands and even your winning hands. You have to think about everything."

We spoke about another friend of ours who went from homeless to millionaire in six months once he found that he had a knack for backgammon. His name was Falafel because at the time that was all he could afford to eat. Ylon told me, "Falafel memorized every statistic about backgammon. Right now on the web you can see that his tournament games are ranked #1 in terms of how accurately they mimic a computer. Falafel also studied every single game he lost."

I used to play Falafel every day in chess. He'd sleep on the ground in Washington Square Park and get up in the morning with dirt and leaves in his hair and we'd play chess for fifty cents a game. Now million dollar bankrolls from backgammon are normal for him.

F) EXPERIENCE.

At some point you have to cook 10,000 meals. Or play a million hands of poker, or 1000s of games of chess. Or start 20 businesses. Very few are successful right away. That would require too much luck and luck favors the prepared and the persistent. In those 1000s of whatever you will encounter much failure. We all know that the best baseball players in the world are enormous successes if they strike out "only" 70% of the time. When my dad died I went to his house and logged onto this chess account. I saw that he played about 30,000 games. He never got any better. A lot of people can play the 10,000 hands of poker and never get better. Or bake 1000 cakes and never get better. You have to remember your experiences, study your failures, try to note what you did right and what you did wrong, and remember them for future experiences. Will future experiences be exactly like the old experiences? Never. But you have to have the ability to say "Hmm, this is like the time four years ago when X, Y, and Z happened."

G) PATTERN RECOGNITION

Being able to recognize when current circumstances are like an experience you had in the past or an experience SOMEONE ELSE you've studied had in the past is critical to mastery. Pattern recognition and mastery is a combination of all of the above: study + history + experience + talent + a new thing…Love.

H) LOVE

Andre Agassi famously says he doesn't love tennis. I believe this and I don't believe it. We all know that there are all kinds of love. There's unconditional love, which is very hard. The Dalai Lama can have unconditional love. Then there's lust. You look at someone and she is the Oomph to your Ugh. She is the BAM! To you BOOM! You dream and daydream and dream and day-dream until the love is all worn out and six months or six years later it's over and you move on. Then there's love that matures. There's a set of things you like about a person, even love. Mix that in with some lust. Then this love mash up changes over time. Or you learn to adapt because you know that a maturing love is not one where you settle or explore the subtleties inside the other person but you are finally able to explore the subtleties inside of yourself. And sometimes you just fall out of love. There is no shame in this. Do what your heart tells you to do.

Some relationships are weird combinations of all of the above. They are tumultuous. There is much pain and much pleasure. Perhaps tennis was like that for Agassi. I can't speak for him. But to become a master at anything there will be much pain. And it can't be avoided. Nobody has avoided it. If something is too much pain, then it's not the worst thing in the world to give up. I don't like dental surgery. It's too much pain for me. So my teeth are messed up a bit. I give up on having perfect teeth.

I) Psychology

One reason most people in the world don't get really good at anything is because they have no talent for anything that anyone cares about. Another reason is they don't want to put in the work. I understand this. Often it's better to be social and have friends and strong family relationships and love people. Many people who have mastered something often have a hard time with their relationships with family members or spouses or friends. Van Gogh cut off his ear. Dostoevsky, Kafka, Bobby Fischer, Godel, were never known for their social skills and often were faced with depression, suicidal tendencies or borderline schizophrenia.

When you have a career, there's this idea that you will go from success to success. You start in the cubicle, then you get an office, then a corner office, then you move horizontally into a CEO position at another company, and so on. You might have some failures along the way but they won't be big failures. With mastery the one thing in common is that there are ALWAYS big failures.

With poker champ Ylon Schwartz, the day before he left for Las Vegas in 2008 where he won over $3 million I was with him, providing support for him in a court case. He had a court appointed attorney because he was dead broke and in debt. He asked me that day, "I have to get on a plane for Las Vegas tomorrow and when I get back I could go to jail. How am I going to get through this?" I didn't have an answer for him other than the usual clichés. But he got on that plane. And every day he went higher and higher in chips. And he won $3.7 million in that tournament and hasn't looked back.

A lot of people in the investing world don't like Tim Sykes. He has a very arrogant marketing style. He's a friend of mine and I can tell you he's not that arrogant. He's extremely humble. The reason he's so humble is that he's gone broke several times since his first success. It's no fun going broke. I've gone broke several times. You never go broke and think, "Well, it didn't work this time, but it will work next time." You go broke and you think, "That was the worst experience in my life and I'd be better off dead. That was my last chance. It's all over for me now. I'd rather be dead than go through this pain I'm feeling right now. And everyone around me would be better off if I were dead." That's what you think. And when Tim was making one of his comebacks, nobody would speak to him. I had him on some videos with the company I was working with but ultimately they banned him. So he chose himself. He did all of the above. I've since looked at his audited track record and seen that he's made millions from trading. I know 1000s of day traders. 1000s. I know one successful day trader and that's Tim.

On the path to Mastery, everything will go wrong. As Robert Greene points out in his book, "Mastery", Napoleon got banished to Elba where he supposedly said his famous palindrome (somehow speaking English for the first and only time in his life) "Able was I ere I saw Elba". Every master has his Elba. Banished to an island where the life you once knew no longer exists and it seems like there is no way to escape. Napoleon escaped because he was the best in the world at what he does. Because he had the psychology, or perhaps the blind spot, to not recognize that this was "it", his final destination. Studying how he came back to power is a great example of psychology mixed with all of the above skills in becoming a master.

Tim went from millions to broke to trading out of his parent's basement to millions again and this time he's not going to fall back.

Bobby Fischer spent much of his life in borderline schizophrenic agony when he couldn't deal with his losses. He'd disappear for years at a time but then come back stronger than ever.

How do you build that psychology? I don't know. It's a combination of many things:

- EGO. A real belief that you *can* be the best, against all possible rational evidence against this. Against everyone trashing you simultaneously.

- NO WAY OUT. I asked Ylon, Lewis, and many others what were they thinking at rock bottom and the answer almost always was: "What else could I do with my life? I had to keep going!"

J) PERSISTENCE

Add up all of the above and you get persistence. Persistence creates luck. Persistence overcomes failure. Persistence gets you experience. Persistence is a sentence of failures punctuated by the briefest of successes, and eventually those successes will start to propel you towards mastery. Not one success or two. But many, many, many.

How do you get persistent when life is filled with changing careers, relationships, responsibilities, economic crashes, historical upswings, and so many things that can get in your way. There's no answer at all. That's why it's called persistence. Because no matter where you are, there you are, doing what you always did. Not letting any of the above stop you. Using all of the above in your Mastery Arsenal to propel you to higher successes and deeper failures and then even higher successes. It's painful and brutal and no fun and nobody will ever understand why. And when you achieve success people will act as if it's the most natural thing in the world to have happened to you. And you try to explain, "No, there was this one time…" but they don't want to hear it. They want to know what their next move should be so they can be where you are.

There's no next move. There's only your next move.

K) MYSTERY

Ultimately, Mastery = Mystery. You're going to break the sound barrier on some field that nobody has ever gone that fast or that far. You're going to find your own unique combination of passions that make you the best in the world at that combination. What if nobody cares? That's ok also. You care. What if you never go for the mystery? What if you settle back into the known, the comfortable, the stress-free existence of your peers and colleagues and everyone you ever knew. The world might not allow it. What you thought was comfortable might've been a myth also.

So you can only do this:

ASK: what can I do right now to move forward. This second. Having a goal in the distant future is almost a damnation of this moment in time. An insult. We can't predict the future. And the history of mastery shows that nobody was able to predict which goals would work and which wouldn't. Only this moment matters. Health-wise: physically, emotionally, mentally, and spiritually. Can you move forward today in each? Then you will attract the mastery and the mystery.

· · · · · · · · · · · · · · · ✳ · · · · · · · · · · · · · · ·

THE GOOD NEWS

You don't have to be the master of the world. You don't have to do any of the above. Very few people do. And many of them experienced much hardship and pain along the way. And will continue to experience that hardship. We live in a culture where it's almost a damnation to be considered mediocre. But society has no clue about what real mastery is. Don't listen to any of the "Top 10 things..." articles. Don't listen to anyone. Not even me. Freud has said that our two goals in life are human connection and achievement. But often it's a reasonable goal to overcome these evolutionary inclinations. To be happy with your loved ones. To be satisfied for every gift in your life, for every moment, not rushing to the next moment of mastery. True mastery can be found right here, right now. Choosing yourself right now in how you treat yourself, how you treat the people around you, how you treat your efforts and your loves. Nothing is more important than this. Nothing compounds into greater happiness in life more than this. Because when you rush to get to a mythical THERE, one day you will arrive and realize you missed all of the pleasures and mysteries along the way.

HOW DOES A RICH EMPLOYEE TRANSFORM ANGER INTO "WHAT WORKS"?

············ ✳ ············

I'm really stupid. I can tell you in advance. I think at heart, if I work at it, I can be smart. But at the moment I'm largely an idiot. I feel I have the right knowledge but I let a lot of stuff get in the way. You know: "stuff". Worries, guilt, paranoia, grudges, resentment. Like, for instance: I resent the people who resent me. I think they resent me for no reason. So now I resent them. What a circle-jerk. I used to think when I added stuff to my brain I'd get smarter. But this is not true. For instance, if I look up when Charlemagne was born I'd just add a fact to my head, which I will forget tomorrow. This won't make me smarter. Subtraction, and not Addition, is what makes the window to the brain more clear, wipes away the smudges, and opens the drapes.

One example: the day I lost the deal to do Tupac's website, I had a chess lesson afterwards. I couldn't play at all. It was like I didn't even know the rules. My instructor said, "what's wrong with you today?" But I was ashamed. And angry at myself. So my intelligence went way down, like 80% down. By the way, just notice when these things come up. It's not like you're going to get cured of paranoia. But notice when it appears. Water withers the rock away. Every time you notice, the window clears a tiny bit. A smudge is gone. You get a glimpse of the light outside.

You get a tiny bit smarter. Maybe later you have to look for the deeper emotional reasons for why you feel the way you do. And there are a lot of reasons. Everyone could've made fun of your acne in junior high school and now you want to be loved by everyone. (Err, maybe that happened to me) But right now, this second, just don't get hit by a car when you cross the street.

You can say: "hey, wait a second! All of those things equal up to more than 100%!" Well, what can I say? You're smarter than me.

So here's my great list.

1) PARANOIA

I figure on the moments when you are paranoid (is she cheating? Is he stealing? Are they talking about me? Will they sue me? Etc.) you lose about 30-50% of your intelligence. That's a big chunk. For me its because I can't think of anything else. I would circle her house until the lights were on and then I'd knock on the door. Or I would go to his office and not leave until he showed up. Paranoia will destroy you.

2) RESENTMENT

Someone wrote about me a year ago. I hold a grudge. He was a friend, and then wrote the worst crap about me. What a jerk. But when I think about it, I figure I lose about 20% of my intelligence. Particularly if the thoughts involve revenge. Then maybe 30% of my intelligence.

3) REGRET

I've written about it a billion times. I lost a lot of money in 2000-2001. I regret it. Or, I should say, I regretted it. I don't anymore. How come? Because I saw that regret was taking at least 60% of my intelligence away. I couldn't afford 60%. 2% I could afford. Not 60%. I didn't start coming up with ideas for new businesses until the regret went away.

4) PERFECTIONISM

When I was running a fund I never wanted to have a down month. I'd be afraid to talk to my investors then. One guy, who is still a good friend (I spoke with him today even) said, "listen, if you're going to be a fund manager you have to be able to talk to people when you have a down month".

But I was ashamed. When I lost my house, I moved 70 miles away. I didn't want to run into anyone. I felt shame. When I write a blog post I think is weak, I might take it down before too many see it. I'm ashamed of it. I want to win the Nobel Prize for blog writing. Or at least 10,000 Facebook likes. But I can't control that. I'm imperfect. The shame of imperfections takes at least 20% of my intelligence away. Because people sense and appreciate honesty and honesty about imperfections, believe it or not, creates enormous opportunities. I've seen it happen in my own life.

5) CONTROL

I want to control everything around me. But sometimes things are bad and there's nothing you can do about it. Sometimes you have to surrender and say, "this is bad now but good things will happen later". Then a great weight lights off your shoulders.

You know why they always say: "a great weight lifts off your shoulders?" because that's where your brain is. And your brain is heavy. It rests on your shoulders. When stuff is weighing it down you lose about 10-20% of your intelligence. Give up control and get smarter. A simple example: you are late for a meeting but there's traffic. You can think "God damn this traffic. Why am I always in traffic?" Or you can be thinking about something smart: like how good bacon tastes. Can I make better bacon? Or how would I start a helicopter airline to take me from one side of the city to the other. These seem like dumb thoughts. But they are much better than "God damn this traffic!"

6) GUILT

A good friend of mine wrote me recently. I should say, wrote me six weeks ago. Every day when I wake up I tell myself: don't return emails until you read, then write. But then sometimes I have other things to do. Meetings. Or BS stuff. Or eating. I say, "ok, I will return that email later." And then when later comes I feel bad that I haven't returned his email earlier. Then at 3am I turn over and say to Claudia, "I didn't return that email". She says "Urgh…ushghsh…emmmm" which was not the answer I was looking for. Then I don't sleep as much. Then I feel guilty. That takes away about 10% of my intelligence right there.

7) WORST CASE SCENARIO

Lets say I lose $1000 in the stock market once day. Sometimes I think to myself, "holy shit, if I lose that amount every day for the next…." And it gets worse and worse. My worst case scenarios has my children begging for food on the harsh streets of Bangalore. I've spent at least a year of my life, when you add it up, thinking of the worst case scenario. Even though the worst case scenario HAS NEVER HAPPENED. Or if it does happen, it was never as bad as I thought it would be. I have a scarcity complex. If I didn't have that then I'd have an "abundance complex". And I firmly believe, abundance follows an abundance complex. So I'm smarter (and wealthier) when I give up that scarcity complex.

8) TALKING

Claudia wanted to say something important to me. But I spoke instead. I imparted my great wisdom on her before she could get a word out. Finally, she forgot what she was going to say. Probably because my words were so wise they were like the Bible. Or like Robert's Rules of Order. Or Strunk & White. That's how wise I am. STRUNK AND WHITE! Extra talking probably takes away at least 15% of my intelligence. Because I could've been listening and learning. Or reading about grammar. Or not getting into an accident when talking on the phone. Sometimes we just have to Shut Up!

9) EXCUSES

Everyone says, "I can't." I can't be a medical professional unless I go to medical school. I can't be a moviemaker unless I raise $10 million to make a movie. I can't marry a super model because I'm ugly. I can't I can't I can't. For every "can't " you should send me $10. I can do all those things, particularly if I have your $10.

Ugh, 9 things. I can't even make this a "ten-lister" as we *pros* call them in the blog biz. Can someone come up with a tenth for me please?

By the way, just notice when these things come up. It's not like you're going to get cured of paranoia. But notice when it appears. Water withers the rock away. Every time you notice, the window clears a tiny bit. A smudge is gone. You get a glimpse of the light outside. You get a tiny bit smarter. Maybe later you have to look for the deeper emotional reasons for why you feel the way you do. And there are a lot of reasons. Everyone could've made fun of your acne in junior high school and now you want to be loved by everyone. (Err, maybe that happened to me) But right now, this second, just don't get hit by a car when you cross the street.

IS THERE A "RIGHT WAY"
TO ASK FOR THINGS THAT THE
RICH EMPLOYEE UTILIZES?

················ ✳ ················

I was afraid to ask my boss for a raise. I was afraid to ask my girlfriend to move out. I was afraid to ask Claudia to marry me. I was afraid to ask Dick Costolo to write the foreword of "Choose Yourself!" I'm always afraid to ask people for favors. Or to do something that would benefit me. So this was the magic technique, in the first two scenarios above: I quit my job (maybe my boss would counteroffer). I moved to another city rather than ask her to move out. He did counter-offer and I stayed. We did remain broken up because it's hard to maintain a relationship in different cities. I don't know if this counts as "asking for something" but it was certainly an "aggressive-passive-aggressive" way to ask for what I really wanted.

I have this tendency to think of myself as a "giver". Even a "super-giver". But it's not true. Sometimes I have to ask. We all live in a society where it's just as important to ask as it is to give. It almost makes me feel like a fraud when I have to ask for something.

When I was in tenth grade I asked Nadine to go out with me. I think she dropped one of her books when she ran away. I took it as a good sign that she didn't give an instant "no" but just ran instead. I was impressed with how athletic she was. The way she darted in and around the swarm of teenagers who were at this point all looking at me. People pray and ask God for things. This is too easy. He doesn't answer and only in movies does he give any sort of sign. And you have about 50-50 odds of getting what you ask for, give or take. One time when I was selling a company I started, I felt I was not entitled to ask for something unless I lied.

For instance, a potential buyer asked me why I wanted to sell.

I said, "Because I think my company is now at a level where it can grow really fast if partnered with a bigger company." HA! What a load of BS. I came up with that one on the fly. But what if I had just said, "I want to make a lot of money and I want you to give it to me." The only real answer. Then what? He didn't buy my company anyway. It's like talking to a girl at a bar. Something I've never been able to successfully do. There's an entire cottage industry of pickup lines that supposedly "work". I hate to say it: but I'm pretty sure none of those lines work. In part, because I've used many of them. And in part, because people aren't like robots. There's no buttons to press and then the robot comes to life. A woman pretty much knows what you want when you go up to her in a bar. Even if you ask nicely, you're just asking for one thing, no matter what vomit comes out of your mouth and into her face.

So I decided to make a catalog of what "Asks" work and what doesn't. You're welcome to share more types of Ask if you want.

THE PASSIVE AGGRESSIVE ASK

Like, if I want something from Claudia but I'm afraid to say it. There's a slight chance that if I'm COMPLETELY SILENT for 48-72 hours then she might guess what I want and then do it.

This technique will ruin your life.

THE "IT DOESN'T HURT TO ASK" TECHNIQUE

This is maybe even worst than the Passive Aggressive Ask. First off, people say "it doesn't hurt to ask" precisely when it does hurt to ask. You've just given them a problem. Now, if they say "no" they feel like a bad guy. And if they say "yes" they will hate you and you will end up not getting what you wanted.

One time someone wanted to guest-post on my blog. He said, "it doesn't hurt to ask". I have never had a guest post on my blog and suggested he would be even better off if he went to a blog that regularly had guest bloggers. He ended up writing an entire post about what a jerk I was. So it did hurt to ask. It didn't hurt me. But it hurt him because it ruins his ability to ask me (or other people) anything in the future. Often when you do the totally unprepared Ask thinking, "it can't hurt" then not only will the person look down on you (hurt), but you also slander yourself (hurt) and ruin your chances of later Asks or friendship or whatever. Only do the "It doesn't hurt to ask" technique if you're ready for a 95% chance of "no" and you're actually willing to be hurt. This leads to:

THE COLD ASK

If you're willing to handle lots of Nos, then ask a lot of people. This is like cold calling. Or asking everyone on the street to have sex with you. Eventually, unless you are me in both the above scenarios, someone will say "yes". In fact, it's good practice to do this Cold Ask in situations where:

A. You don't really care about the person you are asking or what they think of you. "It doesn't hurt"

B. You are asking for something trivially small.

The "cold ask" is a useful technique for another purpose - to practice breaking out of your comfort zone. It's a useful exercise, for instance, to go to a distant mall, stand by an escalator, and ask everyone coming down if they will have coffee with you. This is a good way to break out of the shy comfort zone that so many of us deal with every day. You won't be shy if you do this. I've done it and it works.

BEGGING

You would think begging is the worst. I've tried it. I went down to Wall Street once. I wore a suit. I asked everyone going into the New York Stock Exchange if they would give me $5. Nobody gave me five dollars. One guy got very upset. He said, "no" to me and left and then he came back and said: "What is this for" and he raised his arm as if he was going to hit me. The wrong place to threaten violence is on Wall Street. There are about 5000 police and guard dogs there. So I wasn't worried. I asked about 100 people for $5. One guy gave me money. He had $1. He gave it to me. He was a homeless guy sitting against a wall. Another guy gave me a hot dog.

So Begging works. Why does begging work? Because you're actually giving something to the person you are asking. What are you giving? Status over you.

If I ask Claudia to see the movie "Superbad" for the tenth time and she says no and I say, "PLEASE! PLEASE! COME ON!" then she knows she will gain some status over me if she says "yes" and that she can cash that status at some later point.

For the homeless person on Wall Street, who is so used to having his status trampled on, I gave him a chance to have status over me and he was happy. But for the person, who responds to a Begging Ask, don't forget that Status inflates like a dollar. Over time it becomes worthless so you have to use it while you still can. Remember that, Claudia!

The "If You Do This, I Will Do That" Ask

This 'ask' is pretty bad. If you do this for me, then I'll do X for you later. It's almost like begging but with everything clearly outlined in advance. You would think, this seems fair, it's like bartering. No it isn't. It's more like a bad negotiation where the side being asked is at an unfair disadvantage since he has no time to evaluate the value of what is being bartered. Since abstract things are hard to value on the spot, one side will end up feeling ripped off. Usually the side being Asked.

So you are actually insulting the person you are asking. It won't work.

The "No Pressure" Ask

Now we're starting to get into some decent ask techniques.

If you can truly convey that there's no pressure on them saying "yes" or "no" then you preserve the relationship if they say "no". In fact, in some cases you even make it better.

1. You show that you respect the person's right to say No

2. You can follow up with later No Pressure Asks and even deepen the relationship.

This worked well for me, for instance, when I wanted to sell a company, was told "No" and then was able to follow up with monthly updates for over a year before they got interested again. In fact, I've probably used this technique successfully on many important occasions. It even works in online dating. You stay in the "online friend zone" until lightning strikes. Actually, that's never worked for me but I hear that it does. It's hard to convey "No pressure". Because there's always a tiny bit of pressure. One way to do a no-pressure Ask is to ask for advice.

For instance, I can ask a buyer, "What would you do if you were me and you wanted to sell your company?". Or you can ask a client, "What else would you recommend I do to improve my presentation to ANY client so that I could potentially ask for more business." This is really no pressure. They don't have to respond. Or, they can feel pleased that you give them status (status they rightly deserve) and respect their status so much that you aren't directly asking. It's like they are the sun and you can't stare straight at them. That's the no-pressure Ask.

Often a response in the "no pressure ask" results in you getting more business from the client. They feel flattered and they instantly want to help you.

THE RECIPROCITY ASK

This is the Hare Krishna technique mentioned in Robert Cialdini's book. When the Hare Krishnas asked for money, they would get nothing but NOs. But when they gave a little flower first, they got billions. Once you give something in advance, the brain naturally wants to give back and show that it is a good member of the herd. But here's the trick: if you ask immediately, then I personally think it's a little too slimy. Like the Hare Krishna trick. The key is to do a "Give" and then forget about it. And then a month, a year, a decade later, come back with the "Ask".

A Give creates potential energy in the future. An Ask turns the Potential energy into Kinetic energy. I hope I'm getting that physics analogy right. Create as much potential energy as possible every day with many Gives. Store up your Asks for when you need them.

THE 10X ASK

This is THE most powerful ASK and almost always works. Particularly when combined with the "NO PRESSURE" Ask. A few months ago I flew to visit Amazon and visited many of their departments where they showed me what they were working on. If I had just called them and said, "I want you to spend your whole day showing me what you are doing" I would never have gotten a response. Instead I spent a long amount of time thinking of good ideas I could build or they could build that would help them with one aspect of their business. If they were bad ideas, or if I didn't put the time in, they never would've responded. I gave them value. And I said "no pressure on responding. These are now your ideas for free." A few months later the head of business development called me and invited me to visit. Which I was happy to do. I spent the day at Amazon and then saw the very first Starbucks. It was a simple ask but it involved about ten hours of work on my part plus a lot of experience dealing with subtleties in the Amazon experience.

So maybe about 100 hours worth of work to ask to visit Amazon's headquarters and learn how I can publish books better. If you want someone to spend one hour of their life helping you, then you need to spend 10 hours of your life, at least, helping them IN ADVANCE and with NO PRESSURE. Every ASK that has created immense value in my life, even millions of dollars, was a result of me doing ten times the amount of work first, for free, before I got the door even slightly open.

If you are like me, you feel like you have to give and never ask. Or you feel afraid to ask. Or you are shy to ask. I am shy to the point that sometimes I even cry, I'm so nervous before I ask for a favor. When I asked Claudia to marry me, I probably put in at least a 1000 hours of hard work and sweat. Fortunately, that was enough for her to say "Yes" in one second. But first, she made me promise to let her die first. Well, we'll see if I can live up to that Ask.

As A Rich Employee How Do I Know If I Should Take A Job In A Start-Up?

·············· ✳ ··············

I magine if someone asked: "Would you invest in this company?" Your answer is going to be similar. With a few additions. Here's the checklist I would follow:

A. Has the CEO built a business before?

This is not always reliable (Mark Zuckerberg or Larry Page hadn't built businesses before) but there's an interesting stat: 85% of startups fail. If the CEO has built and sold a startup before then the odds go down to 25%. So you might as well have the statistics on your side.

B. Does the company have good funding?

BY GOOD FUNDING I MEAN TWO THINGS:

A. Enough money to last at least a year.

And, by the way, this is an important thing to note: if the company has six months or less worth of funding THEN THEY ARE ALREADY OUT OF BUSINESS. Which is why "A" above is so important. A good CEOs knows this.

B. "Good funding" means people (or funds) who will also write second checks, meaning, they have the power to help a company if it falls on hard times because they will be able to write a second check. If all they have is one year's worth of friends and family money then you are taking the risk that in a year they will run out of money. Why take risks when there are plenty of other good jobs out there? And, I'll throw in a bonus third thing on this:

C. Do you believe in the vision?

THIS CAN MEAN SEVERAL THINGS.

A. The CEO is creative enough to develop a strong vision and he's also a good enough communicator to convey that vision.

B. You would use the product (if the product was applicable to you)

C. You can't use the product but you can easily see how this product can help a million or more people.

I'LL GIVE A GOOD EXAMPLE AND A BAD EXAMPLE.

GOOD EXAMPLE: Tesla. You would work for Tesla if you believe in Elon Musk's vision of reduced dependence on fossil fuels, or if you want to drive a Tesla, or if you think if everyone driving an electronic car (and having a powerwall) will help a million or more people.

BAD EXAMPLE: someone pitched me an idea where consumers can pick the type of ads they see. I do NOT see how this would really help a million or more people. So I would not work for a company like that (and, by the way, they had a lot of investors). I invested in a startup recently that developed a technology for vaping vitamins and medical drugs. I USE the product (I vape B12 with it, Vitamin D with it, and trans-reservatrol). And I can easily see how this can help a million or more people (the entire US is Vitamin D deficient and people's bodies are unable to digest vitamin pills. (By the way, not trying to get anyone interested in this - already fully funded).

D. Valuation.

You're presumably getting options at a startup and, depending on the value you contribute, those options will increase. How do you know if their latest round valuation is good? Forget for a second the money they raised (we dealt with that above). But imagine you had, in cash, the amount of their full valuation. Would you be able to create a better product with more traction? Like, for $46 billion, would you be able to beat Uber? Unclear to me. But there are plenty of startups out there where if you gave me their full valuation in cash I can easily see how they can be replaced. Don't work for a company that is easily replaceable at a lower valuation. If you believe in the valuation, make sure your options are not at the venture capital price but at the "409A valuation" price. Google that.

E. Learning

There's a great story about Sergey Brin interviewing people. He can usually tell in the first few minutes if he's not going to hire someone. So then he spends the rest of the interview making sure he learns at least one thing from the interviewee Make sure that even in the worst case scenario where you misjudged everything else, that you at least learn one thing fairly quickly after you take the job so that it adds to your skillset and you can move on to get a better job. I took a job once at HBO (not a startup but still) where I learned so much in a three year period I was able to take the skills (ranging from technology to entertainment to TV production) leave and start a successful company.

F. Subtleties

I visit a lot of companies per year for various reasons. I always look for the subtleties.

A. How do the partners get along. For instance, one company I was about to invest in was a co-CEO situation. I heard one of the CEOs gossiping about the other. I didn't invest. The entire culture of a company comes from the top down. So if the partners who started the business don't have their emotional act together, the company itself won't be emotionally sound.

B. How do the employees talk about the clients. Read the biography of the founder of JetBlue. He would stay up to 3 in the morning every night responding to customer service emails. Once a month he would ride on one of the longer plane rides and starting at the back of the plane and moving to the front he would sit with every passenger and ask them if they had any problems with the flight. He actually hired employees that way. That's the CEO but everyone in the company should have that attitude towards customers. A year ago I visited a law firm where they were trashing their customers and making jokes about it. That's not the sort of company I would hire, work for, invest in, etc. A company and its customers are ONE eco-system. Not "us vs. them".

C. Your boss and his/her boss.

A lot of bosses make hiring decisions based on "would you ride in a cross-country airplane next to this guy". You should make your decision the same way about your potential bosses. Believe me — they need you more than you need them. So you have to like them. Also, think ecosystem again - try to see their relationships with other people in the company. All gossiping is bad. Hopefully they think highly of the people they work with. Else you shouldn't work for them and you shouldn't work for that company.

G. Demographic Trends.

Warren Buffett is not a value investor. Everyone thinks he is but he hasn't done real value investing since the early 1960s. Warren Buffett is a demographic investor. Two quotes from Buffett:

"If a company is going to be here 20 years from now then it is probably a good stock to buy".

AND

"If you have a strong demographic wind behind you then the company will do well even with poor management".

EXAMPLE: the book, "Bold" lists a lot of demographic trends that take advantage of Moore's Law that are getting bigger. Robotics, Internet of Things (sensors), 3D Printing, etc. That's one start. Another start is companies disrupting healthcare since that is such a mess right now. Another example: I'd rather work for Uber than a company that lends money against taxi medallions. I'd rather work for AirBnb than Marriott. I'd rather work for Tesla than GM.

H. Light At the End of the Tunnel

You can't ask in your interview, "when will you IPO?" It's unpredictable when a company will "exit" (i.e. get sold or IPO or have some event which allows employees to sell some of their shares). A good company might wait 7-10 years before an exit. In fact, a good company SHOULD wait 7-10 years. How come? Because if they are good then they are undoubtedly growing faster than the market. So they should stay private as long as possible to maximize benefits for shareholders / employees. Here's the problem. The average employee stays at a startup for 3.1 years (perhaps that corresponds to vesting schedules, I don't know). Make sure you can wait for that 7-10 year run. Also, I'd try to figure out if management is ultimately interested in an exit. Some CEOs are not.

I. Eventual Profits.

Make sure you see the path to profitability. Some startups might be years away. But the good thing about working for a company that ultimately has huge margins (not just profits but margins) is that they have a lot of perks. Just compare the chef at Google with the chef at Walmart. Hint: there's IS NO chef at Walmart. This seems like a big checklist before you decide to work for a startup. But don't forget that YOU are the valuable person here. Take care of all of your needs and then you will have more freedom, be able to demonstrate greater competence at your job, and have better relationships with the people you work with. In other words, you'll be happy. And that's a nice reason to take a job.

Resources For The Rich Employee

Create A Choose Yourself Meet-up In Your Town

·············· ✳ ··············

Remember: for me, the way I was able to dig out of every hole I created for myself was by choosing myself. This meant I had to just focus on today. The best predictor (the only predictor) of a successful tomorrow, was a successful today. A successful today simply meant that I focused on 1% improvement each day in my physical health, emotional healthy (being around people who loved and supported me and who I loved and supported), mental health (writing down 10 ideas a day), and spiritual health (always practicing replacing regrets and anxieties with gratitude).

I repeat that a lot. I write about that a lot. But it's because it's the one consistent thing I can track any success in my life to. And it's a practice. It's not a goal. It's something I have to do every day.

One way I am able to keep with a practice every day like this is to associate with other people who are working on similar ways to improve themselves. Really it's not so hard: everyone in an ideal world would like to be healthier in all of the above ways. It's how we fill in the blanks (some people might like tennis, others like cross-fit. Some might like to write ten ideas a day, others like painting, etc.) that might be different, but the results are the same.

I like to meet with my "Choose Yourself Group". People I associate with who have similar goals, who I like, who are willing to share and be open and share their challenges with me while I share mine and maybe we can all help each other. These meetups are invaluable to success.

I highly recommend everyone either join a Choose Yourself meetup (and you can find them at *ChooseYourself.Me* all around the world) or start your own.

Keep it small, keep it simple. Three people in a living-room are more than enough to share weekly on how to keep learning, how to network, how to keep improving by 1% a day.

And note, these meetups are not meetups of entrepreneurs. Or employees. Or people who want to talk about marketing, or where to put the sales letter on a website, or what products to sell. These meetups are for all of the above and then some. We can always choose ourselves no matter what we do. It's about building up that inner energy and then directing it powerfully into outer energy. This is the most powerful energy I have ever encountered in my life.

Choose Yourself Meetups have now sprouted all over the world, and we highly recommend they are small, no more than 30 people, because we all crave sitting in a circle like we did for thousands of years. We crave the intimacy and human warmth of a circle of trust.

These are the guidelines we propose, and we wrote them with only one goal in mind: That you choose yourself to be whatever it is you want to be, today. That you get to be a rich employee or just a happy person, in any area you choose to pursue.

How To Run A Choose Yourself Meet-Up

············ ✳ ············

Remember, when a meeting gets to be too big (more than 30 people) it might be time to split it into two meetings. Meetings can also happen on the phone through free conference calls. I've put a lot of thought into what the ideal components of a "Choose Yourself" meetup would look like. A huge benefit of splitting meetings into smaller groups is that each town can have a variety of meetings at different times and dates hence enabling more and more people to free themselves.

Choosing yourself requires that you make your own networks and connections that can allow you to continue along the themes of your life. Freedom is the result. More calm is the result. Less conflict in your life is the result. A "Choose Yourself" meetup will, over repeated meetings, automatically lend itself to increasing the benefits of doing a daily practice. I encourage anyone to form one and run it. By the end of the meeting, people will reap several benefits:

- Ideas on how they can change up or improve their daily practice.

- Ideas on how they can move away or get less dependent on the gatekeepers in their life.

- Ideas on networking. We all need help from others to succeed, pay our bills, meet our obligations, and move forward. Having the support or even simply meeting people who have a similar mindset would certainly help.

- Human contact. The life of someone who chooses him- or herself can be lonely at times, the meetings can ensure that we socialize and have fun.

So here's what I think an optimal "Choose Yourself" meetup would look like. And by the way, if you recognize some themes from twelve-step meetings of Al-Anon or AA, you are right. Those meetings have been working fine for over one hundred years. The model works, people attend and they benefit, so why not?

By using their models we get hundreds of years of popular consensus on the best ways to get everyone to:

- PARTICIPATE.
- FEEL WELCOME.
- SPEAK UP.
- MINGLE.
- SHARE THEIR OWN STORIES WITHOUT INTERRUPTIONS.
- RESPECT EACH OTHER.
- KEEP GOSSIP OUT.
- HANDLE THE GROUP'S FINANCIALS.
- CHOOSE THEMSELVES.
- IMPROVE THEIR LIVES.

Also, each meeting can, through their own "monthly" or "periodically" business meeting, modify their own format. Each meeting can choose itself; Each group can do its own thing, provided that the members of the group agree on it.

We suggest a meeting of an hour or an hour and a half to start.

At the stipulated time the meeting starts, exactly on time, as this is a sign of respect for everyone's time.

THE FACILITATOR SPEAKS:

Hello, my name is X and today I choose myself. I am the chair for this meeting, and that does not mean I own anything or direct anything, I am just member of the community doing service for a specified period of time.

(At this point a notebook might be passed around with dates of future meetings for people to write down their names for when they are available and willing to chair a meeting.)

THE FACILITATOR CONTINUES:

People attending this meeting are welcome to chair any of our meetings, because when we rotate the leadership, and follow meeting guidelines, we ensure that we put principles before personalities and that we keep the focus on what is important: choosing ourselves for success. In the spirit of camaraderie and for the highest good of all, we do not criticize, gossip, interrupt or talk over each other. We respect the order of the meeting.

We remember to put principles before personalities, and if someone feels uncomfortable at any time, anyone can ask the chair to read this introduction again. Any discussions about changes or improvements to our meetings should be brought up in the business meeting, which for this meetup is held every Xth of the month.

We also do not focus on criticizing, or complaining about people who are not here. We do not blame others or put anyone down. Instead we focus on ideas and healthy partnerships that can help each of us move forward to-

ward creating the life we want. We know that choosing ourselves starts with our own health, and we start with that, with getting to a place of health for us, regardless of other people in our lives.

In short, we put the focus on the life we want to create, and not on regrets of the past. The only purpose of this meeting is to choose ourselves, become idea machines, become healthy spiritually, emotionally, mentally and physically, and help each other surpass gate-keepers that may appear to stand between us and a rewarding and successful life, for today.

The format of the meeting starts with either having someone share their story of choosing themselves for 15 minutes, or reading for fifteen minutes from either Choose Yourself!, The Choose Yourself Guide to Wealth, The Choose Yourself Stories, or The Rich Employee. We remind everyone that whatever is said in this meeting is confidential and must not leave the room. Confidentiality allows all of us to feel safe and share our deepest vulnerabilities. Keeping these meetings confidential is a sign that we are willing to be altruistic, and ready to create a safe space for everyone to choose himself or herself.

Now let's go around the room and introduce ourselves by first name only and share one sentence on something you did during this week to bring the Daily Practice alive. E.g.: "Hi, I'm Mary and this week I've been making lists with ten ideas per day" or "I slept eight hours a day, I spent time with my friends," or "I'm very grateful each day for ten things." If you are a newcomer we welcome you and hope that the meetings can help you as much as they are helping us.

Starting with the facilitator, go around the room.

THE FACILITATOR CONTINUES:

TIMEKEEPER

We need a timekeeper who will be willing to time the fifteen minutes of the reading and later on the three-minute shares. Participation is key to success; if you usually hide by blending with the background we encourage you to try and do service like that of keeping time for others. Do we have a timekeeper?

Thank you, Y, for your service.

Everyone please keep an eye on the timekeeper and respect his or her signals. When the timekeeper says that the time is up please acknowledge his or her and say I will wrap up, and finish, so we can all share.

FIFTEEN-MINUTE READING OR SHARING OR READING

THE FACILITATOR CONTINUES:

Now lets read from [Choose Yourself!/The Choose Yourself Guide to Wealth/The Rich Employee/Choose Yourself Stories]. The book will be passed around and each of us will read two paragraphs. If you do not want to or cannot read, simply pass the book to the next person.

Although we highly encourage your participation, we understand if you simply can't do it for any reason.

OPTION #2

Some groups may opt to change the reading of the book if there is a person who can share their story of how they choose themselves, in that case, the person will speak for fifteen minutes.

FACILITATOR SAYS:

Now we will have a share from a member who is choosing him or herself. There will be no interruptions, no questions and no cross talk. The qualification for a "speaker" or "qualifier" is that she or he has been to at least two meetings of Choose Yourself run as per the guidelines, and is willing to share.

OPTION #3

Once a month, or once every so often, the meetings need to have a business meeting because it is key to maintaining the finances/electing new chairs (for example if the meetings happen monthly and we need a quarterly person to commit to running the scripted meetings) / select a "library person" who will use funds from the treasurer to buy a book if it is needed, select a "treasurer" who will keep track of donations and keep safe any prudent reserve savings and pay the rent (if applicable) etc. The meeting is timed at ten minutes. And it runs like this:

YOU CAN ALSO FOLLOW THE ROBERT'S RULES OF ORDER.

FACILITATOR SAYS:

We need a volunteer to run the business meeting, can someone please volunteer? [wait] Thank you "Z" for your service. Z will read from the format and we will run this business meeting for 15 minutes. The time keeper will let us know when there is only five minutes left and when there is one minute left, are you OK with that timekeeper? Thanks for your service.

OPEN: Read minutes from the last business meetings.

1. Treasurer's report he or she says how much money there is in reserve, if we are on time paying the rent and the meetup fees, etc.

2. Library report: do we need to have a book for new comers? Can we get money from the treasurer to do so?

3. Old Business Followed by New Business: People propose ideas, if one is proposed it needs to be seconded, and then there is discussion and voting. If time is running out things can be tabled for the next meeting

If something is proposed we will have discussion and voting.

DONATIONS

FACILITATOR SAYS:

Now, before we move on to shares we will pass a basket/envelope around for donations. We do have some fees associated with the meetup and the space, and a suggested donation is three to five dollars. But if you cannot do it, we understand, please keep coming back because we need YOU more than your money.

SHARING: Until fifteen minutes before the closing of the meeting, Shares are 3 minutes or 2 minutes each.

FACILITATOR SAYS:

The floor is now open for sharing. Please remember to acknowledge the timekeeper, do not talk about other people in the room and keep your sharing to your own experiences. Cross talk or criticizing is not accepted as we keep the focus on ourselves and we respect the time each person has for

their own share. We share our stories of how we are choosing ourselves and the experiences we encounter along the way. If anyone feels uncomfortable or feels there is cross talk he or she can ask the facilitator to read this again. If anyone wants to give feedback to someone else that can be done in the after meeting, one-on-one.

Fifteen minutes before the meeting ends we will talk about: Gatekeepers, permission networking, and idea sex.

FIVE MINUTES: Gatekeepers

FACILITATOR SAYS:

We are now fifteen minutes from the end of the meeting so we will discuss gatekeepers.

By show of hands people ask permission to speak and the facilitator picks the first person, which in turn, when finished, will pick the next.

If nobody volunteers, then the facilitator can do the first share, or wait until someone wants to share.

FACILITATOR CONTINUES:

If you are experiencing a "gatekeeping" situation you can share it with us and we will listen. There will be no cross talk, but in the after-meeting if anyone cares to share or help one another you can do so.

Volunteers can describe the gatekeepers that are in their way. For instance, they just submitted a book to a publisher. Or they are hoping for a promo-

tion from their boss. There will be no cross talk, and networking is highly encouraged after the meeting.

People will have suggestions but it's hard to follow suggestions. Everyone has to come up with the solutions from inside. By sharing in the open we give each other a chance to form new ideas from within.

If nobody is sharing on this you can continue with the next segment.

FIVE MINUTES: Permission Networking

FACILITATOR SAYS:

Perhaps someone has an idea they want to share with someone at a certain company, or they need a contact. Or maybe someone wants to meet someone from another industry. Or maybe someone wants to meet Richard Branson (space's the limit here). We all have ideas. Some have ideas for themselves, some have ideas for others.

People can simply state: I would like a contact at SalesForce, in the marketing department. Again, no cross talking, if someone is willing to talk to this person the end of the meeting is where these conversations will happen.

If nobody is sharing on this you can continue with the next segment.

FIVE MINUTES: Idea Sex

FACILITATOR SAYS:

Probably when people were sharing their Daily Practice of the week, they shared one or two of their ideas (or more) from their idea-list that week. Imagine taking one of your ideas and combining it with one of their ideas, what would result. Some riffing could occur here but no criticism. Every bad idea is an idea and worth exploring.

Ideas are like mazes. You never really know where you are going until you hit the exit. Even a dead end is an opportunity to turn around and explore more of the maze.

Write down ten ideas that you got just by being on the meeting. After the close people can have idea-sex from what they heard and thought.

CLOSE

FACILITATOR SAYS:

We have now come to the close of the meeting, we are grateful that you are here and we hope you benefit from this gathering. Keep coming back!

THE AFTER-MEETING

There should be at least fifteen to thirty minutes of "after-meeting" where people walk around and talk to one another.

This also gives people a chance to get to know and support one another and to fulfill the second part of the daily practice, which is meeting more and more people who are interested in helping you and supporting you.

RESOURCES

Fedora	Online courses on general topics
TedX	Take online courses from the world's best universities.
Coursera	Take the world's best courses, online, for free.
Coursmos	Take a micro-course anytime you want, on any device.
Highbrow	Get bite-sized daily courses to your inbox.
Skillshare	Online classes and projects that unlock your creativity.
Curious	Grow your skills with online video lessons.
Lynda.com	Learn technology, creative and business skills.
CreativeLive	Take free creative classes from the world's top experts.
Udemy	Learn real world skills online.

Codecademy	Learn to code interactively, for free.
Stuk.io	Learn how to code from scratch.
Udacity	Earn a Nanodegree recognized by industry leaders.
Platzi	Live streaming classes on design, marketing and code.
Learnable	The best way to learn web development.
Code School	Learn to code by doing.
Thinkful	Advance your career with 1-on-1 mentorship.
Code.org	Sart learning today with easy tutorials.
BaseRails	Master Ruby on Rails and other web technologies.
Treehouse	Learn HTML, CSS, iPhone apps & more.
One Month	Learn to code and build web applications in one month.
Dash	Learn to make awesome websites.

············· DATA ·············

DataCamp   Online tutorials and data science courses.

DataQuest   Learn data science in your browser.

DataMonkey   Develop your analytical skills in a simple, yet fun way.

············· LANGUAGES ·············

Duolingo   Learn a language for free.

Lingvist   Learn a language in 200 hours.

Busuu   The free language learning community.

Memrise   Use flashcards to learn vocabulary.

············· FUN ·············

Chesscademy   Learn how to play chess for free.

Pianu   A new way to learn piano online, interactively.

Yousician   Your personal guitar tutor for the digital age.

ClaudiaYoga   Yoga tips for every day life

P.S.: RESOURCES LIST WRITTEN BY @KRISTYNAZDOT,

FOUNDER AND CEO OF MAQTOOB.COM

BOOK SUGGESTIONS

··············· ✳ ···············

"Are You Fully Charged?: The 3 Keys to Energizing Your Work and Life" –By: Tom Rath (or my podcast with him)

"The End of Jobs: Money, Meaning and Freedom Without the 9-to-5" –By: Taylor Pearson (or my podcast with him)

"The Miracle Morning: The Not-So-Obvious Secret Guaranteed to Transform Your Life (Before 8AM)" –By: Hal Elrod

"How Successful People Think: Change Your Thinking, Change Your Life" –By: John Maxwell

"Become an Idea Machine. Because Ideas are The Currency of The 21ˢᵗ Century" –By: Claudia Azula Altucher (yes, my wife's book but filled with great prompts to start the idea machine process)

"The Surrender Experiment: My Journey into Life's Perfection" –By: Michael Singer (how a guy who gave up everything ended up with a billion dollar company)

"The Architecture of Persuasion: How to Write Well-Constructed Sales Letters" –By: Michael Masterson

"Yes!: 50 Scientifically Proven Ways to Be Persuasive" –By: Robert Cialdini

"7 Habits of Highly Effective People" –By: Stephen Covey (I don't think this book will ever be out of date and is a must-read)

"Tomorrowland: Our Journey from Science Fiction to Science Fact" –By: Steven Kotler (to see up close the trends that are heading in our direction as a society)

"StrengthsFinder 2.0" –By: Tom Rath

"Bounce: Mozart, Federer, Picasso, Beckham, and the Science of Success" –By: Mathew Syed (the last two books are about the balance between finding your talents versus finding your strengths)

"The Start-up of You: Adapt to the Future, Invest in Yourself, and Transform Your Career" –By: Reid Hoffman and Ben Casnocha

"Seven Years to Seven Figures: The Fast-Track Plan to Becoming a Millionaire" –By: Michael Masterson

"Mastery" –By: Robert Greene

"A Curious Mind: The Secret to a Bigger Life" –By: Brian Grazer (Grazer is the producer of many great movies and TV shows and, in my opinion, became the ultimate rich employee simply by mastering the art of questioning)

"Quitter" –By: Jon Acuff

"Powers of Two: How Relationships Drive Creativity" –By: Joshua Wolf Shenk

"Lean In: Women, Work, and the Will to Lead" –By: Sheryl Sandberg (despite the focus on women, I think this is a must-read for everyone)

"The War of Art" and *"Turning Pro: Tap Your Inner Power and Create Your Life's Work"* –By: Stephen Pressfield (how we fight the internal resistance to our success)

"The Obstacle Is the Way: The Timeless Art of Turning Trials into Triumph" –By: Ryan Holiday (a modern guide to stoicism)

"80/20 Sales and Marketing: The Definitive Guide to Working Less and Making More" –By: Perry Marshall

"To Sell Is Human: The Surprising Truth About Moving Others" –By: Daniel Pink

"Play It Away: A Workaholic's Cure for Anxiety" by Charlie Hoehn

In Conclusion

· · · · · · · · · · · · · · · ✳ · · · · · · · · · · · · · ·

This is not the end of the journey.

Choosing yourself is the way of the warrior. It's difficult to keep up with a daily practice that will not only change your life but will change the lives of everyone around you.

It doesn't matter if you are an employee or an entrepreneur.

This is the method for finding meaning in your life no matter where you are, and tying that meaning to all of your activities, jobs, and relationships. It's in this manner, that wealth is an automatic byproduct.

My suggestion, and you can take whatever part of this you want:

Read this book and the other *Choose Yourself* books. The books cost 99 cents. I deliberately keep the price at this because I want people to benefit. But I also know that people don't read or value what they don't pay for. Read the books I recommend in the resources section.

Go to a Choose yourself meetup or find Choose Yourself accountability partners.

Join the Choose Yourself group on Facebook. It's free and it's fun. Everyone shares and there are fascinating stories of people who are choosing themselves.

If you wish to read my free daily emails you are more than welcome to. You can sign up for my list, read my blogs, listen to my podcasts, at jamesalt-ucher.com all for free.

Most of all, don't look at your job and think, "the grass is greener over there" where "there" might be some startup, or some day-trading career, or some promotion from vice-president to associate senior vice-president.

There is always "here". Right inside of you, the internal energy that is waiting to explode with more energy than anything seen before.

"Here" is where you make your contribution. Where you get out of your head and start to transform yourself to someone who goes from thinker to Do-er.

"Here" is where joy is.

And, after all is said and done, isn't that what we are here for?

BOOKS IN THE
CHOOSE YOURSELF FAMILY

·············· ✳ ··············

CHOOSE YOURSELF!

THE CHOOSE YOURSELF STORIES

THE CHOOSE YOURSELF GUIDE TO WEALTH

BECOME AN IDEA MACHINE

ABOUT THE AUTHOR

················· ✳ ·················

James Altucher is a writer, successful entrepreneur, angel investor and chess master. He has started and run more than 20 companies and he is invested in over 30.

He writes for major media outlets including the Wall Street Journal, The New York Observer, Yahoo Finance and Tech Crunch. His blog, The Altucher Confidential, has attracted more than 30 million readers since its launch in 2010.

He is the author of 18 books that have been translated into 25 languages combined, including two Wall Street Journal best-sellers: *"Choose Yourself"* and *"The Power of No"*.

His podcasts: 'The James Altucher Show' and 'Ask Altucher', have been downloaded over 20 million times.

James is a Ted Talk Speaker (TEDx San Diego 2014), a Linked In Influencer, and a Quora Top Writer 2014 and 2015. Join him at JamesAltucher.com or on Twitter @Jaltucher.

CONTACT

··············· ✳ ···············

T ext James your questions to: **203.512.2161.**

That is his *personal* cell phone.

Please don't call him because he NEVER picks up the phone nor does he have a voicemail. If you text him he might respond right away or your question may be featured on an episode of Ask Altucher

Join Him Weekly on His Twitter Q&A.

Every Thursday from 3:30 to 4:30 PM EST, you can Tweet him questions on anything at @Jaltucher and he will respond, live.

WSJ BEST SELLING AUTHOR OF
CHOOSE YOURSELF!

THE RICH

EMPLOYEE

JAMES ALTUCHER

Made in the USA
San Bernardino, CA
07 September 2015